Breads
& Muffins

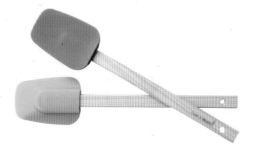

THE AUSTRALIAN
Women's Weekly

contents

I don't think there is anything more comforting than the smell of home-made bread straight from the oven. We've taken this a step further, and developed a wide array of breads, sweet and savoury, from around the world for you to try at home; your house will be filled with moreish breads so you're sure to become a bread addict, just like me. From pizza dough to naan bread, hot cross buns and scones, we're certain that this book will keep you (and the kids) entertained for hours.

Pamela Clark
Food Director

onion focaccia

preparation time 20 minutes (plus standing time) cooking time 25 minutes (plus cooling time) serves 8

2½ cups (375g) plain flour

2 teaspoons (7g) dried yeast

¼ cup (20g) grated parmesan cheese

2 tablespoons coarsely chopped fresh sage

3 teaspoons sea salt flakes

1 cup (250ml) warm water

¼ cup (60ml) olive oil

1 small white onion (80g), sliced thinly

1 Sift flour in large bowl; stir in yeast, cheese, sage and 1 teaspoon of the salt. Gradually stir in the water and 2 tablespoons of the oil. Knead on well-floured surface about 10 minutes or until smooth and elastic.

2 Place on greased oven tray; press into a 24cm-round. Cover with greased plastic wrap; stand in warm place until dough doubles in size.

3 Preheat oven to 220°C/200°C fan-forced.

4 Meanwhile, combine onion, remaining salt and remaining oil in small bowl. Remove plastic wrap from dough; sprinkle dough with onion mixture. Bake, uncovered, in oven about 25 minutes or until cooked when tested; cool on wire rack.

PER SERVING *8.2g fat; 999kJ (239 cal)*

ITALIAN BREADS

olive bread

preparation time 45 minutes (plus standing time) cooking time 1 hour serves 12

2 teaspoons (7g) dried yeast

1 teaspoon caster sugar

1¼ cups (310ml) warm milk

3⅓ cups (500g) plain flour

1 teaspoon salt

¼ cup (60ml) extra-virgin olive oil

1 cup (120g) seeded black olives, chopped finely

1 Combine yeast, sugar and milk in small jug; stand in warm place about 15 minutes or until mixture is frothy.

2 Sift flour and salt into large bowl. Stir in yeast mixture and oil; mix to a firm dough. Knead dough on floured surface about 5 minutes or until smooth and elastic. Place dough in oiled bowl; cover, stand in warm place about 1½ hours or until dough has doubled in size.

3 Turn dough onto lightly floured surface; knead until smooth. Press dough into 23cm x 28cm rectangle. Spread olives over dough, leaving a 2cm border. Roll up dough from long side, tuck ends underneath; place on lightly greased oven tray.

4 Sift a little extra flour over bread. Using scissors, make cuts about 2.5cm apart, along centre of bread. Place bread in warm place; stand, uncovered, about 1 hour or until doubled in size.

5 Meanwhile, preheat oven to 180°C/160°C fan-forced.

6 Bake in oven about 1 hour or until bread is browned and sounds hollow when tapped. Serve with butter, is desired.
PER SERVING *6.2g fat; 899kJ (215 cal)*

TIP Bread is best made on day of serving.

olive, anchovy and caper bruschetta

preparation time 15 minutes cooking time 5 minutes serves 8

½ loaf ciabatta (275g)

3 cloves garlic, halved

⅓ cup (80ml) olive oil

3 anchovy fillets, drained, chopped finely

½ cup (60g) seeded black olives, chopped finely

1 tablespoon drained baby capers

1 tablespoon lemon juice

⅓ cup (25g) parmesan cheese flakes

2 tablespoons marjoram

1 Cut ciabatta into 1.5cm-thick slices; halve any large slices crossways. Toast under hot grill until browned lightly; while still hot, rub one side of toast with garlic. Place toast in single layer on tray; drizzle ¼ cup (60ml) of the oil evenly over toast. (Can be made three hours ahead to this stage and covered.)

2 Combine anchovy, olives, capers, juice and remaining oil in small bowl.

3 Just before serving, divide olive mixture among bruschetta; top with cheese then marjoram.

PER SERVING *11.3g fat; 792kJ (189 cal)*

tomato and rocket bruschetta

preparation time 15 minutes cooking time 5 minutes serves 8

½ loaf ciabatta (275g)

3 cloves garlic, halved

¼ cup (60ml) olive oil

3 medium egg tomatoes (225g), chopped finely

½ small red onion (50g), chopped finely

25g baby rocket leaves

1 Cut ciabatta into 1.5cm-thick slices; halve any large slices crossways. Toast under hot grill until browned lightly; while still hot, rub one side of toast with garlic. Place toast in single layer on tray; drizzle oil evenly over toast. (Can be made three hours ahead to this stage and covered.)

2 Combine tomato and onion in small bowl.

3 Just before serving, top bruschetta with tomato mixture, then rocket; sprinkle with freshly ground black pepper, if desired.

PER SERVING *7.8g fat; 628kJ (150 cal)*

napoletana pizza

preparation time 20 minutes (plus standing time) cooking time 30 minutes serves 6

300g mozzarella cheese, sliced thinly

¼ cup coarsely torn basil leaves

BASIC PIZZA DOUGH

2 teaspoons (7g) instant yeast

½ teaspoon salt

2½ cups (375g) plain flour

1 cup (250ml) warm water

1 tablespoon olive oil

BASIC TOMATO PIZZA SAUCE

1 tablespoon olive oil

1 small white onion (80g), chopped finely

2 cloves garlic, crushed

425g canned crushed tomatoes

¼ cup (70g) tomato paste

1 teaspoon white sugar

1 tablespoon fresh oregano

1 Halve basic pizza dough; roll out each half on lightly floured surface to form 30cm round. Place on two oiled pizza trays. Spread each with half of the basic tomato pizza sauce; top with cheese.

2 Preheat oven to 220°C/200°C fan-forced.

3 Bake, uncovered, in oven about 15 minutes or until crust is golden and cheese is bubbling. Sprinkle each with basil before serving.

BASIC PIZZA DOUGH Combine yeast, salt and sifted flour in large bowl; mix well. Gradually stir in the water and oil. Knead on well-floured surface about 10 minutes or until smooth and elastic. Place dough in large oiled bowl; stand in warm place about 30 minutes or until dough doubles in size. Knead dough on lightly floured surface until smooth. Roll out dough as required or to fit pizza tray.

BASIC TOMATO PIZZA SAUCE Heat oil in medium frying pan; cook onion, stirring occasionally, over low heat until soft and transparent. Stir in garlic, undrained tomatoes, paste, sugar and oregano. Simmer, uncovered, about 15 minutes or until mixture thickens. (Can be made two days ahead and refrigerated, covered, or frozen for up to six months.)

PER SERVING *18.1g fat; 1890kJ (452 cal)*

TIPS Purchased pizza bases can be used in place of the basic pizza dough. Basic pizza dough can be made three hours ahead and refrigerated, covered. Remove from refrigerator 10 minutes before using.

olive bread with oregano

preparation time 25 minutes (plus standing time) **cooking time** 45 minutes (plus cooling time) **serves** 10

1 tablespoon dried yeast

1 teaspoon white sugar

2¼ cups (560ml) skim milk

5½ cups (825g) plain flour

⅓ cup (80ml) olive oil

1¼ cups (150g) seeded black olives, halved

2 tablespoons coarsely chopped fresh oregano

1 Combine yeast, sugar and milk in large bowl; stir in 3 cups (450g) of the flour. Cover; stand in warm place 30 minutes or until foamy. Stir in oil, then remaining flour. Knead on floured surface about 10 minutes or until smooth and elastic. Place dough in large oiled bowl. Cover; stand in warm place until doubled in size.

2 Meanwhile, drain olives on absorbent paper.

3 Preheat oven to 200°C/180°C fan-forced.

4 Turn dough onto floured surface; knead in olives and oregano. Roll dough into 30cm x 35cm oval; fold almost in half. Place on large greased oven tray; sift 2 tablespoons of plain flour over dough.

5 Bake, uncovered, in oven about 45 minutes or until cooked when tested; cool on wire rack. Serve with sliced cheese and tomato, if desired.
PER SERVING *8.5g fat; 1632kJ (390 cal)*

TIP Bread can be made a day ahead and then warmed before serving.

pagnotta

preparation time 25 minutes (plus standing time) **cooking time** 40 minutes (plus cooling time) **serves** 6

2 teaspoons dried yeast

½ teaspoon white sugar

2 teaspoons salt

3½ cups (525g) plain flour

1¼ cups (310ml) skim milk, warmed

1 tablespoon olive oil

1 Combine yeast, sugar, salt and flour in large bowl. Gradually stir in milk and half of the oil until combined.

2 Knead dough on lightly floured surface about 2 minutes or until well combined. Place dough in large oiled bowl; turn to coat in oil. Cover; stand in warm place about 30 minutes or until dough doubles in size.

3 Turn dough onto floured surface; knead 10 minutes or until dough is smooth and elastic. Shape dough into 58cm log; place on an oiled and floured oven tray. Lightly brush ends with water; gently press together to form a ring. Combine remaining oil and 2 teaspoons warm water in small bowl; brush over dough. Sift over a little extra plain flour.

4 Place in cold oven; turn temperature to 200°C/180°C fan-forced. Bake, uncovered, about 40 minutes or until cooked when tested; cool on wire rack. Serve with jam, if desired.
PER SERVING *4.2g fat; 1471kJ (351 cal)*

cheese breadsticks

preparation time 30 minutes (plus standing time) cooking time 10 minutes (plus cooling time) makes 40

60g butter, melted

1 teaspoon dried yeast

2 tablespoons olive oil

2 teaspoons white sugar

½ teaspoon salt

1¼ cups (100g) grated parmesan cheese

¾ (180ml) cup warm water

2½ cups (375g) plain flour

1 Combine butter, yeast, oil, sugar, salt, cheese and the water in large bowl; gradually stir in flour. Knead on lightly floured surface about 10 minutes or until smooth and elastic. Place dough in large oiled bowl; turn to coat in oil. Stand in warm place 10 minutes.

2 Preheat oven to 220°C/200°C fan-forced.

3 Cut dough into quarters; roll each quarter into 10 logs, about 20cm long. Place 1cm apart on lightly greased oven trays.

4 Bake, uncovered, in oven about 20 minutes or until crisp and browned; allow to cool on wire racks.
PER BREADSTICK *3.1g fat; 266kJ (63 cal)*

STORE Breadsticks can be kept in an airtight container for two weeks.

roasted capsicum and prosciutto bruschetta

preparation time 20 minutes cooking time 7 minutes serves 8

½ loaf ciabatta (275g)

3 cloves garlic, halved

¼ cup (60ml) olive oil

2 medium red capsicums (400g)

5 prosciutto slices (75g), chopped coarsely

1 tablespoon balsamic vinegar

2 tablespoons fresh oregano

1   Cut ciabatta into 1.5cm-thick slices; halve any large slices crossways. Toast under hot grill until browned lightly; while still hot, rub one side of toast with garlic. Place toast in single layer on tray; drizzle oil evenly over toast. (Can be made three hours ahead to this stage and covered.)

2   Quarter capsicums; remove and discard seeds and membranes. Place capsicum on oven tray; roast under hot grill or in very hot oven, skin-side up, until skin blisters and blackens. Cover capsicum pieces in plastic 5 minutes. Peel away skin; discard. Cut capsicum into thin strips.

3   Cook prosciutto in medium heated oiled frying pan until crisp. Add capsicum and vinegar to pan; stir to combine. Cool to room temperature.

4   Just before serving divide capsicum mixture among bruschetta; top with oregano.
    PER SERVING *8.4g fat; 695kJ (166 cal)*

creamy mushroom bruschetta

preparation time 20 minutes cooking time 15 minutes serves 8

½ loaf ciabatta (275g)

4 cloves garlic, halved

½ cup (125ml) olive oil

250g flat mushrooms, chopped finely

1 tablespoon lemon juice

½ cup (125ml) cream

125g button mushrooms, sliced thinly

2 tablespoons finely grated parmesan cheese

¼ cup coarsely chopped fresh chives

1   Cut ciabatta into 1.5cm-thick slices; halve any large slices crossways. Toast under hot grill until browned lightly; while still hot, rub one side of toast with three cloves of the garlic. Place toast in single layer on tray; drizzle half of the oil evenly over toast. (Can be made three hours ahead to this stage and covered.)

2   Crush remaining garlic. Heat remaining oil in medium frying pan; cook flat mushrooms, stirring over heat, until very soft. Add juice; stir over high heat until absorbed. Pour in cream; stir to combine. Gently stir in button mushrooms; stir over high heat until almost all liquid is absorbed. Remove from heat; stir in cheese.

3   Just before serving, top bruschetta with mushroom mixture, and then sprinkle with chives.
    PER SERVING *22.7g fat; 1221kJ (292 cal)*

tomato and mushroom calzone

preparation time 45 minutes (plus standing time) cooking time 1 hour (plus cooling time) serves 4

2 teaspoons (7g) dried yeast

½ teaspoon white sugar

½ cup (125ml) warm water

1 cup (150g) plain flour

½ cup (75g) polenta

½ teaspoon salt

2 tablespoons olive oil

1 tablespoon polenta, extra

TOMATO SAUCE

1 tablespoon olive oil

1 medium brown onion (150g), chopped finely

2 cloves garlic, crushed

425g canned crushed tomatoes

¼ cup (70g) tomato paste

1 teaspoon white sugar

1 tablespoon finely chopped fresh oregano

2 teaspoons finely chopped fresh thyme

MUSHROOM FILLING

1 tablespoon olive oil

150g flat mushrooms, chopped finely

12 drained artichoke hearts, halved

2 tablespoons drained capers, chopped finely

1 tablespoon finely chopped fresh dill

1 Lightly oil 30cm pizza pan.

2 Combine yeast, sugar and the water in medium bowl; stand about 10 minutes or until frothy.

3 Combine flour, polenta and salt in large bowl; stir in yeast mixture and oil. Mix to a firm dough.

4 Knead dough on floured surface about 8 minutes or until smooth and elastic. Roll dough until large enough to fit prepared pan.

5 Place dough on pan; spread with tomato sauce, leaving 3cm border.

6 Spoon mushroom filling over half of the dough; brush border with water. Fold over other half to enclose filling; fold edge to seal. Sprinkle with the extra polenta.

7 Preheat oven to 200°C/180°C fan-forced.

8 Stand calzone in warm place about 10 minutes or until risen. Bake in oven about 35 minutes or until browned.

TOMATO SAUCE Heat oil in large saucepan; cook onion and garlic, stirring, until onion is soft. Add undrained tomatoes and remaining ingredients. Simmer, uncovered, about 15 minutes or until mixture is thickened; cool.

MUSHROOM FILLING Heat oil in large saucepan; cook mushrooms, stirring, until browned lightly and liquid has evaporated. Stir in artichokes, capers and dill.

FISH OPTION Sprinkle non-vegetarians' portions with chopped smoked salmon before folding dough over to enclose filling.

PER SERVING 20g fat; 1881kJ (449 cal)

TIP Tomato sauce and mushroom filling can be made a day ahead and refrigerated, covered, separately; tomato sauce suitable to freeze.

vegetarian calzone

preparation time 1 hour (plus standing time) cooking time 35 minutes serves 4

2 teaspoons (7g) dried yeast

1 teaspoon white sugar

1½ cups (375ml) warm water

4 cups (600g) plain flour

1 teaspoon salt

½ teaspoon cracked black pepper

2 tablespoons olive oil

1 cup (125g) coarsely grated cheddar cheese

VEGETABLE FILLING

1 small eggplant (230g), chopped coarsely

1 tablespoon olive oil

1 large brown onion (200g), chopped coarsely

2 cloves garlic, crushed

1 medium red capsicum (200g), chopped coarsely

2 medium zucchini (240g), chopped coarsely

2 trimmed celery sticks (200g), chopped coarsely

2 tablespoons tomato paste

½ cup (125ml) vegetable stock

1 Whisk yeast, sugar and the water together in small bowl, cover; stand in warm place for about 10 minutes or until the mixture is frothy.

2 Place flour, salt and pepper in large bowl, stir in yeast mixture and oil; mix to a firm dough. Turn dough onto floured surface; knead about 10 minutes or until smooth and elastic. Place dough in large oiled bowl, cover; stand in warm place about 45 minutes or until doubled in size.

3 Preheat oven to 220°/200°C fan-forced.

4 Transfer dough to floured surface; knead until smooth. Divide the dough into 4 pieces; roll each piece to a 24cm round. Spread one side of each round with a quarter of the filling; top with a quarter of the cheese. Fold each round in half to enclose filling; press edges together. Place calzone on oiled oven trays; brush with a little extra oil. Cut 2 small slits on top of each calzone; bake, uncovered, in oven about 20 minutes or until browned.

5 VEGETABLE FILLING Place eggplant in strainer, sprinkle with salt; stand 30 minutes. Rinse eggplant under cold water; drain on absorbent paper. Heat oil in large pan; cook onion and garlic, stirring, until onion is soft. Add eggplant, capsicum, zucchini and celery; cook, stirring, about 5 minutes or until vegetables are soft. Add paste and stock; cook, stirring, until mixture thickens; cool. (Can be prepared ahead to this stage. Cover; refrigerate overnight or freeze.)

PER SERVING 26.8g fat; 3574kJ (855cal)

potato focaccia

preparation time 25 minutes (plus standing time) cooking time 25 minutes serves 4

2 cups (300g) plain flour

½ teaspoon salt

2 teaspoons (7g) dried yeast

2 tablespoons olive oil

1 cup (250ml) warm water

1 large potato (300g), sliced thinly

1 tablespoon fresh rosemary

1 clove garlic, sliced thinly

1 Place flour, salt and yeast in large bowl. Gradually stir in oil and water, mix to a soft dough. Knead dough on floured surface about 5 minutes or until smooth and elastic. Place dough onto oiled oven tray; press into 24cm round. Cover loosely with plastic wrap; stand in warm place about 1 hour or until doubled in size.

2 Preheat oven to 220°C/200°C fan-forced.

3 Remove plastic wrap from dough; top with potato then sprinkle with rosemary and garlic. Bake in oven about 25 minutes or until focaccia is just browned and sounds hollow when tapped. (Can be made ahead to this stage. Cover; refrigerate overnight.) Just before serving, place focaccia under hot grill about 3 minutes or until top is crisp.

PER SERVING 10.2g fat; 1680kJ (402cal)

potato and rosemary pizza

preparation time 8 minutes cooking time 15 minutes serves 4

For this recipe we used packaged pizza bases, which measure 15cm across and come in packs of two, but any fresh or frozen variety would also be suitable.

4 x 112g pizza bases

1½ cups (120g) finely grated parmesan cheese

3 tiny new potatoes (120g)

1 tablespoon coarsely chopped fresh rosemary

3 cloves garlic, sliced thinly

1 Preheat oven to 220°C/200°C fan-forced. Place pizza bases on oven tray.
2 Divide half of the cheese into four portions; sprinkle a portion over each pizza base.
3 Slice potatoes thinly using vegetable peeler; divide into four portions. Layer a portion of potato over cheese-topped base in circular pattern until covered; repeat with remaining potato and bases. Divide rosemary and garlic among bases. Sprinkle remaining cheese evenly over pizzas.
4 Bake, uncovered, in oven about 15 minutes or until pizza tops are browned lightly and bases are crisp.
PER SERVING 9.8g fat; 647kJ (155 cal)

TIP You could use one large packaged pizza base instead of making individual servings.

lentil and spinach chapati

preparation time 45 minutes cooking time 40 minutes makes 8

1½ cups (225g) white plain flour

½ cup (80g) wholemeal plain flour

1 teaspoon salt

1 tablespoon vegetable oil

¾ cup (180ml) warm water, approximately

LENTIL AND SPINACH FILLING

1 tablespoon vegetable oil

1 medium brown onion (150g), chopped

2 cloves garlic, crushed

1 teaspoon ground cumin

1 teaspoon garam masala

1½ teaspoons black mustard seeds

½ teaspoon ground turmeric

½ cup (100g) masoor dhal (red lentils), washed, drained

2 cups (500ml) chicken stock

½ bunch (250g) English spinach, finely shredded

1   Sift both flours and salt into large bowl; add oil and enough water to make a firm dough. Knead dough on a floured surface for about 10 minutes or until smooth and elastic; cover dough with plastic wrap, stand 1 hour.

2   Divide dough into 16 pieces; roll each piece, on a floured surface, into a 14cm round chapati. Layer all chapati, separated by plastic wrap, into a stack; cover with cloth.

3   Spread filling over 8 of the chapati, leaving a 1cm border on each; brush border with water. Top each with one of the remaining chapati, pressing edges together to seal.

4   Heat griddle or dry heavy-based frying pan; cook filled chapati, one at a time, until browned on both sides. Keep each chapati warm while cooking the   remainder.

LENTIL AND SPINACH FILLING Heat oil in medium pan; cook onion and garlic, stirring, until onion is browned lightly. Add spices; cook, stirring, until fragrant. Add dhal and stock; simmer, uncovered, about 20 minutes or until dhal is tender and all liquid absorbed. Add spinach; cool.

PER CHAPATI 5.9g fat; 974kJ (233 cal)

TIP These are eaten, in the hand, as a snack in India or served, topped with a thin, soupy dhal and yogurt, as a light meal.

INDIAN BREADS

paratha with kumara and potato filling

preparation time 40 minutes (plus standing time) cooking time 45 minutes makes 8

1½ cups (240g) wholemeal plain flour

1½ cups (225g) white plain flour

1 teaspoon salt

2 tablespoons ghee, melted

1 cup (250ml) water, approximately

¼ cup (60ml) vegetable oil

KUMARA AND POTATO FILLING

400g kumara, chopped

1 tablespoon vegetable oil

1 teaspoon salt

2 teaspoons cumin seeds

2 teaspoons black mustard seeds

2 small potatoes (240g), chopped finely

¾ cup (180ml) water

1 Process flours, salt, ghee and enough water until dough forms a ball. Knead dough on floured surface 10 minutes or until smooth and elastic; cover with plastic wrap, stand 1 hour.

2 Make kumara and potato filling.

3 Divide dough into 16 pieces; roll each piece, on a floured surface, into a 14cm round paratha. Layer paratha, separated by plastic wrap, into a stack.

4 Spread filling over 8 paratha, leaving 1cm border on each; brush border with water. Top each with one of the remaining paratha, pressing edges together to seal.

5 Heat oil in large frying pan; cook filled paratha, one at a time, until browned on both sides. Drain on absorbent paper; keep warm while cooking remainder.

KUMARA AND POTATO FILLING Boil, steam or microwave the kumara until tender; drain, then mash. Heat oil in a medium saucepan; cook salt and seeds, stirring, until seeds pop. Add potatoes and water; cook, stirring, 10 minutes or until potatoes are just tender. Stir kumara into potato mixture; cool.

PER PARATHA 14.9 fat; 1572kJ (376 cal)

maize roti

preparation time 35 minutes (plus standing time) cooking time 20 minutes makes 12

Corn, called makki, is grown mainly in the colder northern areas of India. This fragrant griddle-fried bread is made with pureed fresh corn; you will need about 3 cobs for this recipe.

2 cups (280g) fresh corn kernels

2 teaspoons cumin seeds

1 teaspoon salt

1 tablespoon chopped fresh coriander

1½ cups (225g) plain flour, approximately

1 tablespoon vegetable oil

1 Blend or process corn, cumin and salt until pureed. Transfer mixture to large bowl, stir in coriander.

2 Stir in sifted flour, gradually, until mixture forms a soft dough. Drizzle oil onto dough; mix until no longer sticky.

3 Knead dough on floured surface for about 5 minutes or until smooth; cover with cloth, stand 30 minutes.

4 Divide dough into 12 pieces; roll each piece, on a floured surface, into a 16cm round roti. Layer roti, separated by plastic wrap, into a stack; cover with cloth, stand 10 minutes.

5 Heat griddle pan or dry heavy-based frying pan until very hot; cook roti, one at a time, until just golden brown on both sides. Keep roti warm while cooking remainder.
PER ROTI *2.4g fat; 523kJ (125 cal)*

puri

preparation time 35 minutes (plus standing time) cooking time 15 minutes makes 8

Puri are generally made from the same dough as chapati but are deep-fried in oil rather than dry-fried on a tawa (a cast-iron griddle). They are usually served as part of a thali, a selection of small serves of four or five vegetarian dishes.

1½ cups (240g) wholemeal plain flour

1½ cups (225g) white plain flour

1 teaspoon salt

2 tablespoons ghee, melted

1 cup (250ml) water, approximately

vegetable oil, for deep-frying

1 Process flours, salt, ghee and enough water until dough forms a ball.

2 Knead dough on floured surface for about 10 minutes or until the dough is smooth and elastic; cover with plastic wrap, stand 1 hour.

3 Divide the dough into 8 pieces; roll each piece, on a floured surface, into a 14cm round puri.

4 Deep-fry puri, in batches, in hot oil until puffed and browned; drain on absorbent paper.
PER PURI *9.9g fat; 1150kJ (275 cal)*

besani roti

preparation time 30 minutes (plus refrigeration time) cooking time 20 minutes makes 12

1 cup (140g) besan (chickpea flour)

1 cup (160g) wholemeal plain flour

1 cup (140g) plain white flour

1 teaspoon salt

3 tablespoons ghee

¾ cup (180ml) warm water, approximately

125g ghee, melted, extra, optional

1 Sift flours and salt into a medium bowl, rub in ghee; mix in enough water to make a firm dough. Knead dough on a floured surface 5 minutes or until smooth; cover, refrigerate 30 minutes.

2 Divide dough into 12 pieces; roll each piece, on a floured surface, into a 17cm round roti.

3 Brush roti on each side with extra ghee; cook, one at a time, on a heated tawa or dry frying pan, until brown on both sides. Keep roti warm while cooking remainder. Serve brushed with more melted ghee, if desired.
PER ROTI *14.5g fat; 1041kJ (249 cal)*

naan

preparation time 45 minutes (plus standing time) cooking time 15 minutes makes 6

Naan is that delicious leavened bread we associate with the tandoori dishes of northern India. There, it is baked pressed against the inside wall of a heated tandoor (brick oven).

⅔ cup (160ml) warm water

1 teaspoon dried yeast

1 teaspoon white sugar

2 cups (300g) plain white flour

1 teaspoon salt

⅓ cup ghee, melted

2 tablespoons yogurt

2 teaspoons kalonji (black onion seeds)

1 Whisk water, yeast and sugar in small bowl until yeast is dissolved; cover, stand in warm place 10 minutes.

2 Sift flour and salt into large bowl; add yeast mixture, half the ghee and yogurt. Mix to a soft dough then knead, on floured surface, about 5 minutes or until dough is smooth and elastic.

3 Place dough in large greased bowl; cover, stand in warm place for about 1½ hours or until the dough is doubled in size.

4 Punch down dough; knead on a floured surface for 5 minutes. Divide dough into 6 pieces; roll each piece into a 20cm round naan.

5 Cover oven tray with foil; grease foil. Cook naan, one at a time, under very hot grill for about 2 minutes each side or until puffed and just browned. Brush naan with a little of the remaining ghee, sprinkle with some of the kalonji; grill further 30 seconds. Keep naan warm while cooking remainder.
PER NAAN *12.8g fat; 1229kJ (294 cal)*

walnut and raisin loaf with brie

preparation time 10 minutes cooking time 35 minutes (plus cooling time) serves 8

⅓ cup (55g) raisins

90g butter

½ cup (100g) firmly packed brown sugar

⅓ cup (80ml) water

½ teaspoon bicarbonate of soda

2 eggs, beaten lightly

½ cup (60g) chopped walnuts

½ cup (75g) plain flour

½ cup (75g) self-raising flour

200g brie cheese

1 large bunch grapes (550g)

1 Combine raisins, butter, sugar and the water in medium saucepan; bring to a boil. Remove from heat; stir in soda. Transfer to medium bowl; cool 15 minutes.

2 Preheat oven to 150°C/130°C fan-forced. Grease 8cm x 25cm bar cake pan; line base with baking paper.

3 Stir egg and nuts into raisin mixture; stir in sifted flours. Pour mixture into prepared pan. Bake in oven about 35 minutes or until cooked when tested by inserting a metal skewer into the loaf. Turn onto wire rack to cool.

4 Serve sliced with brie and grapes.
PER SERVING 23.3g fat; 1566kJ (374 cal)

TIP This recipe can be made a day ahead and is suitable to freeze.

LOAVES

fig jam and raisin loaf

preparation time 20 minutes cooking time 50 minutes (plus cooling time) serves 20

125g butter

½ cup (100g) firmly packed brown sugar

2 eggs

1½ cups (225g) self-raising flour

½ cup (160g) fig jam

1 cup (170g) chopped raisins

½ cup (125ml) milk

1 Preheat oven to 180°C/160°C fan-forced. Grease two 8cm x 19cm nut roll tins, line bases with baking paper. Place tins upright on oven tray.

2 Beat butter and sugar in small bowl with electric mixer until light and fluffy. Add eggs, one at a time, beating until just combined between additions (mixture may curdle). Transfer mixture to medium bowl. Stir in flour, jam, raisins and milk, in two batches.

3 Spoon mixture into prepared tins; replace lids.

4 Bake loaves, tins standing upright, in oven about 50 minutes.

5 Stand loaves 5 minutes, remove ends (top and bottom); shake tins gently to release fruit loaves onto wire rack to cool. Serve with jam, if desired.
PER SERVING 6.1g fat; 686kJ (164 cal)

TIPS There are several different sizes and types of nut roll tins available, and it is important that you do not fill them with too much mixture. As a loose guide, the tins should be filled just a little over halfway. Some nut roll tins open along the side; be certain these are closed properly before baking. Some lids have tiny holes in them to allow steam to escape; make sure these are not used on the bottom of the tins. Well-cleaned fruit juice cans may be used instead of the nut roll tins; use a double thickness of foil as a substitute for the lids.

STORE Store fruit loaves in an airtight container for up to three days. Fruit loaves can be frozen for up to three months.

hot cross buns

preparation time 1 hour (plus standing time) cooking time 25 minutes (plus cooling time) makes 16

Although these delicious Easter treats are now served on Good Friday, in olden times they were thought to have holy powers and were present in many religious observances.

2 x 7g sachets granulated yeast

¼ cup (55g) caster sugar

1½ cups (375ml) warm milk

4 cups (600g) plain flour

1 teaspoon mixed spice

½ teaspoon ground cinnamon

60g butter

1 egg

¾ cup (120g) sultanas

FLOUR PASTE FOR CROSSES

½ cup (75g) plain flour

2 teaspoons caster sugar

⅓ cup (80ml) water, approximately

GLAZE

1 tablespoon caster sugar

1 teaspoon gelatine

1 tablespoon water

1 Combine yeast, sugar and milk in small bowl or jug; cover, stand in warm place about 10 minutes or until mixture is frothy.

2 Sift flour and spices into large bowl, rub in butter. Stir in yeast mixture, egg and sultanas; mix to a soft sticky dough. Cover; stand in warm place about 45 minutes or until dough has doubled in size.

3 Grease 23cm square slab cake pan.

4 Turn dough onto floured surface, knead about 5 minutes or until smooth. Divide dough into 16 pieces, knead into balls. Place balls into prepared pan; cover, stand in warm place about 10 minutes or until buns have risen to top of pan.

5 Meanwhile, preheat oven to 220°C/200C fan-forced.

6 Place flour paste for crosses in piping bag fitted with small plain tube; pipe crosses on buns.

7 Bake buns in oven about 20 minutes or until well browned. Turn buns onto wire rack, brush tops with hot glaze; cool. Serve with butter, if desired.

FLOUR PASTE FOR CROSSES Combine flour and sugar in bowl. Gradually blend in enough of the water to form a smooth paste.

GLAZE Combine ingredients in small saucepan; stir over heat, without boiling, until sugar and gelatine are dissolved.

PER BUN 4.9g fat; 1024kJ (245 cal)

STORE Store buns in an airtight container for up to two days. Uncooked buns suitable to freeze for up to three months.

LOAVES

36

gingerbread loaves

preparation time 35 minutes cooking time 25 minutes (plus cooling time) makes 16

200g butter, softened

1¼ cups (275g) caster sugar

¾ cup (270g) treacle

2 eggs

3 cups (450g) plain flour

1½ tablespoons ground ginger

3 teaspoons mixed spice

1 teaspoon bicarbonate of soda

¾ cup (180ml) milk

VANILLA ICING

3 cups (500g) icing sugar

2 teaspoons butter, softened

½ teaspoon vanilla extract

⅓ cup (80ml) milk

1   Preheat oven to 180°C/160°C fan-forced. Grease two eight-hole (½-cup/125ml) petite loaf pans, or line 22 muffin pans (⅓-cup/80ml) with paper cases.

2   Beat butter and sugar in small bowl with electric mixer until light and fluffy. Pour in treacle, beat 3 minutes. Add eggs, one at a time, beating until just combined after each addition. Transfer mixture to large bowl. Stir in sifted dry ingredients, then milk. Divide mixture among prepared pans.

3   Bake in oven about 25 minutes. Stand 5 minutes before turning onto wire rack to cool.

4   Spread icing over loaves; stand until set.
VANILLA ICING Sift icing sugar into heatproof bowl; stir in butter, vanilla and milk to form a smooth paste. Place bowl over simmering water; stir until icing is a spreadable consistency.
PER LOAF 12.4g fat; 1914kJ (458 cal)

TIPS Icing suitable to microwave.
STORE Store cakes in airtight container for up to four days. Uniced cakes suitable to freeze for up to three months.

date and walnut loaf

preparation time 15 minutes cooking time 50 minutes (plus cooling time) serves 20

60g butter

1 cup (250ml) boiling water

1 cup (180g) finely chopped dried dates

½ teaspoon bicarbonate of soda

1 cup (220g) firmly packed brown sugar

2 cups (300g) self-raising flour

½ cup (60g) coarsely chopped walnuts

1 egg, beaten lightly

1 Preheat oven to 180°C/160°C fan-forced. Grease two 8cm x 19cm nut roll tins; line bases with baking paper. Place tins upright on oven tray.

2 Combine butter and the water in medium saucepan; stir over low heat until butter melts.

3 Transfer mixture to large bowl; stir in dates and soda, then sugar, flour, nuts and egg.

4 Spoon mixture into prepared tins; replace lids.

5 Bake loaves, tins standing upright, in oven about 50 minutes.

6 Stand loaves 5 minutes, remove ends (top and bottom); shake tins gently to release nut loaves onto wire rack to cool. Serve with butter, if desired.
PER LOAF *5g fat; 702kJ (168 cal)*

TIPS There are several different sizes and types of nut roll tins available, and it is important that you do not fill them with too much mixture. As a loose guide, the tins should be filled just a little over halfway. Some nut roll tins open along the side; be certain these are closed properly before baking. Some lids have tiny holes in them to allow steam to escape; make sure these are not used on the bottom of the tins. Well-cleaned fruit juice cans may be used instead of the nut roll tins; use a double thickness of foil as a substitute for the lids.
STORE Store nut loaves in an airtight container for up to three days. Nut loaves can be frozen for up to three months.

buttery apple cinnamon loaves

preparation time 10 minutes **cooking time** 25 minutes (plus cooling time) **makes** 8

125g butter, softened

1 teaspoon vanilla extract

¾ cup (165g) caster sugar

2 eggs

¾ cup (110g) self-raising flour

¼ cup (35g) plain flour

⅓ cup (80ml) apple juice

1 small red apple (130g)

1½ tablespoons demerara sugar

¼ teaspoon ground cinnamon

1 Preheat oven to 180°C/160°C fan-forced. Grease eight-hole (½-cup/125ml) petite loaf pan.

2 Beat butter, extract and sugar in small bowl with electric mixer until light and fluffy. Add eggs, one at a time, beating until just combined between additions.

3 Fold in combined sifted flours and juice in two batches. Spread mixture into prepared pans.

4 Cut the unpeeled apple into quarters; remove core, slice thinly. Overlap apple slices on top of cakes.

5 Combine demerara sugar and cinnamon in small bowl; sprinkle half the sugar mixture over cakes.

6 Bake in oven about 25 minutes. Turn cakes onto wire rack to cool. Sprinkle with remaining sugar mixture.
PER LOAF *14.4g fat; 1267kJ (303 cal)*

TIP The cake mixture can also be cooked in texas muffin pans.
STORE Store cakes in airtight container for up to three days. Suitable to freeze for up to three months.

rosemary damper

preparation time 20 minutes cooking time 45 minutes makes 1 loaf

60g butter

1 medium brown onion (150g), chopped finely

3 cups (450g) self-raising flour

2 tablespoons finely chopped fresh rosemary

1 cup (125g) grated tasty cheese

1¼ cups (310ml) water, approximately

1 Melt 15g of the butter in small frying pan. Cook onion, stirring over medium heat about 2 minutes or until onion is soft; cool.

2 Sift flour into large bowl; rub in remaining butter. Stir in onion mixture, rosemary and ⅔ cup of the cheese; make well in centre. Stir in enough of the water to mix to a soft dough; knead on lightly floured surface until smooth.

3 Preheat oven to 180°C/160°C fan-forced.

4 Place dough onto greased oven tray; pat into 16cm circle. Using sharp knife, cut 1cm deep cross in top of dough. Brush with a little extra milk; sprinkle with remaining cheese.

5 Bake, uncovered, in oven about 40 minutes or until damper is golden brown and sounds hollow when tapped.
PER LOAF *97g fat; 10494kJ (2508 cal)*

TIP Damper can be made three hours ahead and stored at room temperature, or frozen up to two months.

cornbread

preparation time 25 minutes (plus standing time) cooking time 20 minutes makes 1 loaf

2 teaspoons (7g) dried yeast

½ cup (125ml) warm water

½ cup (125ml) warm milk

2 cups (300g) plain flour

½ cup (85g) polenta

½ teaspoon salt

2 teaspoons polenta, extra

1 Mix yeast with the water in small bowl; stir in milk. Sift flour into large bowl; stir in polenta and salt. Stir in yeast mixture; mix to a firm dough. Knead dough on floured surface about 10 minutes or until dough is smooth and elastic; place dough in greased large bowl. Cover; stand in warm place about 1 hour or until doubled in size.

2 Preheat oven to 200°C/180°C fan-forced.

3 Turn dough onto floured surface; knead further 5 minutes. Shape dough into 13cm round; place on lightly greased oven tray. Using sharp knife, cut 1cm-deep cross into top of dough. Stand, covered, in warm place 20 minutes; sprinkle with extra polenta.

4 Bake, uncovered, in oven about 20 minutes or until bread sounds hollow when tapped. Serve with butter, if desired.
   PER LOAF *10.7g fat; 1017kJ (243 cal)*

STORE Can be made three hours ahead and stored at room temperature.

beer bread

preparation time 20 minutes cooking time 50 minutes makes 1 loaf

3¼ cups (485g) self-raising flour

2 teaspoons salt

2 teaspoons white sugar

375ml bottle light beer

1 Preheat oven to 180°C/160°C fan-forced. Grease 14cm x 21cm loaf pan; line base with baking paper.

2 Sift flour, salt and sugar into medium bowl; make well in centre. Pour in beer all at once; using spoon, mix to a soft, sticky dough.

3 Knead dough on floured surface until smooth; divide in half. Knead each half; place in prepared pan.

4 Bake, uncovered, in oven about 50 minutes or until bread is browned and sounds hollow when tapped. Turn onto wire rack; serve warm or cold. Serve with sliced tomato and salad greens, if desired.
   PER LOAF *5.8g fat; 7132kJ (1704 cal)*

STORE Can be made three hours ahead and stored at room temperature.

irish soda bread

preparation time 10 minutes cooking time 50 minutes makes 1 loaf

---

2⅔ cups (420g) wholemeal plain flour ·

2½ cups (375g) white plain flour

1 teaspoon salt

1 teaspoon bicarbonate of soda

2¾ cups (680ml) buttermilk, approximately

1 Preheat oven to 180°C/160°C fan-forced.

2 Sift flours, salt and soda into large bowl; return husks from sieve to bowl. Stir in enough of the buttermilk to mix to a firm dough.

3 Knead dough on floured surface until just smooth. Shape dough into 20cm round; place on greased oven tray.

4 Using sharp knife, cut 1cm-deep cross into top of dough. Bake, uncovered, in oven about 50 minutes. Lift onto wire rack to cool. Serve with butter and jam, if desired.
   PER LOAF *27.5g fat; 12746kJ (3046 cal)*

apricot loaf

preparation time 15 minutes cooking time 1 hour 25 minutes (plus cooling time) serves 8

200g dried apricots, chopped coarsely

½ cup (125ml) apricot nectar

½ cup (110g) caster sugar

½ cup (110g) firmly packed brown sugar

250g butter, chopped

3 eggs, beaten lightly

1 cup (150g) plain flour

¾ cup (110g) self-raising flour

1 Preheat oven to 150°C/130°C fan-forced. Grease 14cm x 21cm loaf pan; line base and sides with baking paper, bringing paper 2cm above sides of pan.

2 Place apricots, nectar and sugars in medium saucepan. Bring to a boil then simmer, covered, 5 minutes, stirring occasionally. Remove from heat; add butter, stir until melted. Transfer mixture to large bowl; cover, cool to room temperature.

3 Stir egg and sifted plain and self-raising flours into apricot mixture and spread into prepared pan.

4 Bake about 1¼ hours. Cover hot cake tightly with foil; cool in pan. Serve with butter, if desired.
   PER SERVING *28g fat; 2258kJ (540 cal)*

   TIP This loaf is delicious served warm, spread with butter.
   STORE Cake can be made two days ahead, keep, covered, in airtight container. Cake suitable to freeze for up to three months.

cheese and olive loaf

preparation time 15 minutes cooking time 35 minutes serves 6

1 cup (150g) self-raising flour

⅔ cup (50g) coarsely grated parmesan cheese

2 tablespoons coarsely chopped fresh mint

½ teaspoon ground black pepper

1 cup (120g) black olives, chopped coarsely

75g mortadella, chopped coarsely

4 eggs, beaten lightly

80g butter, melted

1 Preheat oven to 200°C/180°C fan-forced. Lightly grease 8cm x 26cm bar cake pan.

2 Sift flour into medium bowl, add cheese, mint, pepper, olives and mortadella.

3 Add egg and butter; stir until well combined. Spread mixture into pan; bake in oven about 35 minutes or until browned lightly. Turn onto wire rack to cool.

PER SERVING *21.3g fat; 1371kJ (328 cal)*

TIPS Recipe can be made a day ahead; keep, covered, in refrigerator.
STORE Loaf suitable to freeze.

spinach and fetta damper

preparation time 20 minutes cooking time 40 minutes serves 6

3½ cups (525g) self-raising flour

1 teaspoon salt

2 teaspoons cracked black pepper

1 tablespoon white sugar

40g butter

200g fetta cheese, crumbled

200g baby spinach leaves, chopped finely

½ cup (125ml) buttermilk

1 cup (250ml) water, approximately

1 Combine flour, salt, pepper and sugar in large bowl; rub in butter.

2 Stir in cheese, spinach, buttermilk and enough of the water to make a soft, sticky dough.

3 Turn dough onto floured surface; knead until just smooth. Divide dough in half; place in greased disposable baking dish. Press each half into a 10cm round. Cut a cross in dough; about 1cm deep. Brush with a little extra buttermilk, then sift a little extra flour over dough.

4 Cook in covered barbecue, using indirect heat, following manufacturer's instructions, about 40 minutes or until cooked.

PER SERVING *14.8g fat; 1951kJ (466 cal)*

croissants with prosciutto and fontina

preparation time 10 minutes cooking time 10 minutes serves 4

4 croissants

2 teaspoons olive oil

8 slices prosciutto (120g)

½ cup (50g) coarsely grated fontina cheese

100g semi-dried tomatoes, drained, sliced thinly

30g baby rocket

1 Preheat oven to 160°C/140°C fan-forced.

2 Split croissants in half horizontally, without separating; place on oven tray. Heat, uncovered, in oven about 5 minutes.

3 Meanwhile, heat oil in small frying pan; cook prosciutto about 5 minutes or until crisp. Drain on absorbent paper.

4 Place equal amounts of cheese inside croissants; cook, uncovered, in oven about 5 minutes or until cheese melts. Fill croissants with prosciutto, tomato and rocket.

PER SERVING 25.7g fat; 1853kJ (443 cal)

SERVE AS

nectarines on brioche

preparation time 15 minutes cooking time 5 minutes serves 4

4 nectarines (680g)

40g butter, chopped

¼ cup (55g) firmly packed brown sugar

¼ teaspoon ground nutmeg

200g mascarpone

1 tablespoon icing sugar

1 tablespoon Cointreau

2 teaspoons finely grated orange rind

2 small brioche (200g)

2 teaspoons icing sugar, extra

1 Halve nectarines; cut each half into thirds.

2 Melt butter in medium frying pan; add sugar and nutmeg, stir until sugar dissolves. Add nectarines; cook, stirring, until browned lightly.

3 Meanwhile, combine mascarpone, icing sugar, liqueur and rind in small bowl. Cut each brioche into 4 slices; toast until browned lightly both sides.

4 Divide brioche slices among serving plates; top with mascarpone mixture and nectarine pieces. Dust with extra sifted icing sugar.
PER SERVING *43g fat; 2679kJ (640 cal)*

TIP Cointreau is a clear orange-flavoured brandy.

french toast

preparation time 5 minutes cooking time 10 minutes serves 4

3 eggs, beaten lightly

⅓ cup (80ml) cream

⅓ cup (80ml) milk

¼ teaspoon ground cinnamon

1 tablespoon caster sugar

12 x 2cm slices french bread stick

50g butter

1 Combine egg, cream, milk, cinnamon and sugar in large bowl. Dip bread slices into egg mixture.

2 Melt half of the butter in large frying pan; cook half of the bread slices until browned both sides. Repeat with remaining butter and bread. Serve sprinkled with sifted icing sugar, if desired.

PER SERVING *25.1g fat; 1505kJ (359 cal)*

TIP This recipe is best made close to serving.

french toast with berry compote

preparation time 15 minutes cooking time 10 minutes serves 4

4 eggs

½ cup (125ml) cream

¼ cup (60ml) milk

1 teaspoon finely grated orange rind

1 teaspoon ground cinnamon

¼ cup (85g) honey

100g butter, melted

8 thick slices sourdough bread (320g)

¼ cup (40g) icing sugar

BERRY COMPOTE

1 teaspoon arrowroot

⅓ cup (80ml) water

2 cups (300g) frozen mixed berries

2 tablespoons caster sugar

1 tablespoon finely grated orange rind

1 Break eggs into medium bowl, whisk lightly; whisk in cream, milk, rind, cinnamon and honey.

2 Heat about a quarter of the butter in medium frying pan. Dip two bread slices into egg mixture, one at a time; cook, uncovered, until browned both sides. Remove both slices of French toast from pan; cover to keep warm. Repeat with remaining butter, bread slices and egg mixture.

3 Sieve French toast with icing sugar; serve with warm berry compote.
BERRY COMPOTE Blend arrowroot with the water in small saucepan until smooth; add remaining ingredients. Cook until mixture almost boils and thickens slightly.
PER SERVING *42.4g fat; 3154kJ (753 cal)*

TIP Serve with freshly whipped cream.

bagel chips

preparation time 10 minutes cooking time 15 minutes (plus cooling time) makes 40

4 bagels

3 teaspoons peanut oil

2 cloves garlic, crushed

½ teaspoon dried oregano

1 Preheat oven to 160°C/140°C fan-forced.

2 Using serrated or electric knife, cut bagels into very thin slices. Place slices in single layer on oven trays; brush lightly on one side of each slice with combined oil, garlic and oregano.

3 Bake, uncovered, in oven about 15 minutes or until browned lightly; turn chips out onto trays, allow to cool.
PER SERVING *5.3g fat; 1481kJ (354 cal)*

STORE Bagel chips can be made one month ahead and stored in an airtight container.

olive tapenade and mozzarella turkish bread

preparation time 10 minutes cooking time 10 minutes serves 4

⅔ cup (80g) seeded black olives

2 tablespoons finely chopped flat-leaf parsley

2 teaspoons grated lemon rind

1 tablespoon lemon juice

1 clove garlic, crushed

2 tablespoons drained capers

40cm loaf turkish bread

250g mozzarella cheese, sliced thinly

1 Blend or process olives, parsley, lemon rind, lemon juice, garlic and capers until almost smooth.

2 Place bread on oven tray. Spread top with olive tapenade; top with cheese.

3 Cook in covered barbecue, using indirect heat, following manufacturer's instructions, about 10 minutes or until cheese melts and is browned lightly.
PER SERVING *16.2g fat; 1720kJ (411 cal)*

pesto bread

preparation time 10 minutes cooking time 5 minutes serves 6

We used bottled basil pesto and char-grilled vegetable pesto, available from most supermarkets.

40cm loaf ciabatta

¼ cup (60ml) olive oil

¼ cup (65g) basil pesto

¼ cup (65g) char-grilled vegetable pesto

1 Cut bread diagonally into 12 slices. Brush bread slices lightly with oil.
2 Cook bread on heated oiled barbecue, uncovered, until toasted lightly on both sides.
3 Spread half of the slices with basil pesto; spread remaining slices with char-grilled vegetable pesto.
   PER SERVING *19.3g fat; 1577kJ (377 cal)*

bruschetta

preparation time 15 minutes cooking time 5 minutes serves 6

2 large tomatoes (500g), chopped coarsely

1 small red onion (100g), chopped finely

1 clove garlic, crushed

2 tablespoons olive oil

½ teaspoon white sugar

2 tablespoons shredded fresh basil

40cm loaf ciabatta

¼ cup (60ml) olive oil, extra

1 Combine tomato, onion, garlic, oil, sugar and basil in medium bowl.
2 Cut bread into 1.5cm-thick slices; drizzle with extra oil. Cook bread on heated oiled barbecue, uncovered, until toasted lightly on both sides.
3 Serve tomato mixture on toasted bread.
   PER SERVING *17.7g fat; 1554kJ (371 cal)*

SERVE AS

baked ricottas with roasted tomatoes

preparation time 10 minutes cooking time 45 minutes makes 4

2 tablespoons olive oil

2 cloves garlic, crushed

¼ cup (40g) pine nuts

150g baby spinach leaves, chopped coarsely

2 medium tomatoes (380g)

400g ricotta cheese

2 eggs, beaten lightly

⅔ cup (50g) finely grated parmesan cheese

2 tablespoons finely chopped fresh chives

1 Preheat oven to 220°C/200°C fan-forced. Grease four holes of six-hole texas (¾ cup/180ml) muffin pan.

2 Heat half of the oil in medium frying pan, cook garlic and nuts over low heat, stirring constantly, until nuts start to brown lightly. Add spinach; cook, covered, about 2 minutes or until spinach wilts. Cook, uncovered, about 2 minutes or until liquid evaporates. Remove from heat.

3 Cut each tomato into eight wedges; place in medium baking dish, drizzle with remaining oil. Roast, uncovered, 20 minutes.

4 Meanwhile, combine ricotta, eggs, parmesan and chives in large bowl with spinach mixture. Divide mixture among holes in prepared pan.

5 Bake, uncovered, in oven about 20 minutes or until ricottas are firm. Serve baked ricottas with roasted tomatoes.
PER RICOTTA *34.3g fat; 1711kJ (409 cal)*

SAVOURY MUFFINS

triple-cheese muffins

preparation time 10 minutes cooking time 20 minutes serves 4

1 cup (150g) self-raising flour

½ teaspoon bicarbonate of soda

¼ teaspoon cayenne pepper

2 eggs

1¼ cups (310ml) milk

20g butter, melted

4 green onions, chopped finely

2 tablespoons finely grated mozzarella cheese

2 tablespoons finely grated parmesan cheese

2 tablespoons finely grated cheddar cheese

1 Preheat oven to 220°C/200°C fan-forced. Lightly grease eight holes of 12-hole (⅓ cup/80ml) muffin pan.
2 Combine flour, soda and cayenne in medium bowl. Break eggs in small bowl, whisk lightly; whisk in milk, butter and onion until combined. Pour egg mixture into flour mixture; whisk until batter is smooth. Divide half of the batter among prepared holes; top with combined cheeses then remaining batter.
3 Bake, uncovered, in oven about 20 minutes or until muffins are well risen.
   PER SERVING *15.1g fat; 1334kJ (319 cal)*

mini muffin dampers

preparation time 10 minutes cooking time 25 minutes makes 12

3 cups (450g) self-raising flour

40g butter, chopped coarsely

1¾ cups (430ml) buttermilk

2 tablespoons basil pesto

¾ cup (90g) coarsely grated cheddar cheese

¼ teaspoon sweet paprika

1 tablespoon plain flour

1 Preheat oven to 200°C/180°C fan-forced. Grease a 12-hole ⅓-cup (80ml) muffin pan.
2 Place self-raising flour in large bowl; rub in butter with fingertips. Using fork, stir in buttermilk to form a soft, sticky dough. Swirl pesto and cheese through; do not over-mix.
3 Divide mixture among holes of prepared pan. Sprinkle with combined paprika and plain flour.
4 Bake in oven for 25 minutes.
5 Stand dampers in pan 5 minutes before turning out onto wire rack.
   PER DAMPER *7.8g fat; 929kJ (222 cal)*

   TIP Use bottled pesto to save time. If you prefer, a sun-dried tomato pesto can also be used.

bacon and fresh herb muffins

preparation time 15 minutes cooking time 25 minutes (plus cooling time) makes 12

6 bacon rashers, chopped finely

3 cups (450g) self-raising flour

60g butter, chopped coarsely

1 tablespoon coarsely chopped fresh basil

2 tablespoons coarsely chopped fresh chives

2 teaspoons coarsely chopped fresh oregano

¾ cup (60g) grated parmesan cheese

2 eggs, beaten lightly

1 cup (250ml) milk

1 Preheat oven to 200°C/180°C fan-forced.
2 Cook bacon in small frying pan until crisp. Drain on absorbent paper; cool.
3 Place flour in large bowl; rub in butter. Add bacon, herbs and cheese, then combined eggs and milk. Mix using fork until ingredients are just combined; do not over-mix. Mixture should be coarse and lumpy.
4 Divide mixture into greased 12-hole (⅓ cup/80ml) muffin pan. Bake in oven for 20 minutes. Turn onto wire racks to cool.
PER MUFFIN 9.5g fat; 1010kJ (241 cal)

STORE Muffins can be kept in airtight container two days or frozen for up to two months.

chilli cornbread muffins

preparation time 10 minutes cooking time 15 minutes makes 36

1 tablespoon olive oil

4 green onions, chopped finely

¼ cup finely chopped fresh coriander

½ small red capsicum (75g), chopped finely

1 clove garlic, crushed

2 red thai chillies, chopped finely

½ teaspoon ground cumin

1 cup (170g) polenta

½ cup (75g) self-raising flour

½ teaspoon bicarbonate of soda

1 egg

½ cup (125ml) buttermilk

60g butter, melted

CORIANDER CREAM

¾ cup (180ml) light sour cream

½ teaspoon sambal oelek

1 tablespoon finely chopped fresh coriander

1 green onion, chopped finely

1 Preheat oven to 200°C/180°C fan-forced.
2 Heat oil in medium saucepan; cook onion, coriander, capsicum, garlic, chilli and cumin, stirring, until capsicum is soft. Transfer to large bowl.
3 Stir in polenta, flour and soda; stir in combined remaining ingredients. Spoon mixture into three greased 12-hole (1 tablespoon) mini muffin pans.
4 Bake, uncovered, in oven about 10 minutes or until browned.
5 Turn muffins onto wire racks to cool; serve with coriander cream.
CORIANDER CREAM Combine ingredients in small bowl. (Can be made one day ahead and refrigerated, covered.)
PER MUFFIN 3.2g fat; 232kJ (55 cal)

STORE Muffins can be frozen up to six months.

cheese scones

preparation time 10 minutes cooking time 20 minutes makes 24

1½ cups (225g) self-raising flour

¼ teaspoon ground cayenne pepper

2 teaspoons white sugar

⅓ cup (25g) finely grated parmesan cheese

1 cup (120g) coarsely grated cheddar cheese

1 cup (250ml) milk

40g butter, melted

CHIVE BUTTER

60g butter, softened

1 tablespoon finely chopped fresh chives

1 Combine flour, cayenne, sugar, parmesan and half of the cheddar in medium bowl; pour in milk, stir until mixture makes a sticky dough.

2 Preheat oven to 220°C/200°C fan-forced. Lightly oil and flour 20cm round pan.

3 Gently knead dough, until smooth, on a floured surface. Using one hand, flatten dough until about an even 2cm thickness. Using 3.5cm round cutter, cut rounds from dough. Place rounds, slightly touching, in pan.

4 Brush scones with butter; sprinkle with remaining cheddar. Bake, uncovered, in oven about 20 minutes or until browned lightly; turn onto wire rack.

5 Serve warm with chive butter.

CHIVE BUTTER Combine ingredients in small bowl.

PER SCONE *6g fat; 398kJ (95 cal)*

SAVOURY SCONES

little crusty cheese and mustard scones

preparation time 30 minutes cooking time 15 minutes makes 14

4 cups (600g) self-raising flour

1 teaspoon dry mustard

30g butter

2 cups (500ml) milk, approximately

TOPPING

30g butter

2 tablespoons wholegrain mustard

½ teaspoon cayenne pepper

1½ cups (120g) coarsely grated parmesan cheese

1 Preheat oven to 220°C/200°C fan-forced.

2 Sift flour and mustard into large bowl, rub in butter. Stir in enough milk to mix to a soft, sticky dough.

3 Turn dough onto floured surface, knead until smooth. Press dough out to about 1.5cm thickness, cut into 7cm rounds. Place rounds, just touching, onto greased oven trays; sprinkle with topping.

4 Bake in oven for about 15 minutes.

TOPPING Melt butter in small pan, stir in remaining ingredients.

PER SCONE *8.3g fat; 1020kJ (244 cal)*

bacon, egg and mustard scones

preparation time 30 minutes cooking time 20 minutes makes 16

2 rindless bacon rashers (140g), finely chopped

2¼ cups (335g) self-raising flour

90g butter, chopped

2 hard-boiled eggs, finely chopped

¼ cup (20g) finely grated parmesan cheese

2 tablespoons chopped fresh chives

1 tablespoon wholegrain mustard

1 cup (250ml) milk, approximately

2 tablespoons finely grated parmesan cheese, extra

1 Preheat oven to 240°C/220°C fan-forced.

2 Grease 23cm round sandwich cake pan. Cook bacon in pan, stirring, until crisp; drain, cool.

3 Sift flour into medium bowl, rub in butter. Add bacon, eggs, cheese, chives and mustard, stir in enough milk to mix to a soft, sticky dough.

4 Turn dough onto floured surface, knead until smooth. Press dough out to 2cm thickness, cut into 5cm rounds. Place rounds into prepared pan, brush with a little extra milk, sprinkle with extra cheese.

5 Bake in oven for about 15 minutes.
PER SCONE 8g fat; 669kJ (160 cal)

sage and pastrami scones

preparation time 25 minutes cooking time 20 minutes makes 12

1½ cups (225g) white self-raising flour

½ cup (80g) wholemeal self-raising flour

15g butter

2 tablespoons chopped fresh sage

60g pastrami, chopped

1 cup (250ml) milk, approximately

1 Preheat oven to 220°C/200°C fan-forced. Grease 20cm round sandwich cake pan.

2 Sift flours into medium bowl, rub in butter; stir in sage and pastrami. Stir in enough milk to mix to a soft, sticky dough.

3 Turn dough onto floured surface, knead until smooth. Press dough out to 2cm thickness, cut into 5cm rounds, place into prepared pan.

4 Bake in oven for about 20 minutes.
   PER SCONE *2.5g fat; 489kJ (117 cal)*

smoked salmon and sour cream scones

preparation time 30 minutes cooking time 15 minutes makes 12

2 cups (300g) self-raising flour

150g smoked salmon, chopped

⅓ cup chopped fresh dill tips

¼ teaspoon ground black pepper

⅓ cup (80ml) sour cream

1 cup (250ml) buttermilk, approximately

DILL CREAM

½ cup (125ml) sour cream

¼ cup chopped fresh dill tips

1 Preheat oven to 240°C/220°C fan-forced. Grease 19cm x 29cm rectangular slice pan.

2 Sift flour into medium bowl, stir in salmon, dill and pepper, then sour cream and enough buttermilk to mix to a soft, sticky dough.

3 Turn dough onto floured surface, knead until smooth. Press dough out to 2cm thickness, cut into 5.5cm rounds, place into prepared pan.

4 Bake in oven for about 15 minutes. Serve with dill cream.
   DILL CREAM Combine ingredients in small bowl; mix well.
   PER SERVING *8.2g fat; 748kJ (179 cal)*

fruit scrolls with spiced yogurt

preparation time 10 minutes cooking time 25 minutes serves 4

40g butter

¼ teaspoon ground nutmeg

1½ tablespoons brown sugar

1 tablespoon ground cinnamon

1 small apple (130g), peeled, cored, grated coarsely

⅓ cup (50g) finely chopped dried apricots

½ cup (125ml) orange juice

1 sheet ready-rolled puff pastry

½ cup (140g) plain yogurt

1 tablespoon honey

1 Preheat oven to 200°C/180°C fan-forced. Lightly grease oven tray.
2 Melt half of the butter in small saucepan; add nutmeg, sugar and half of the cinnamon. Cook, stirring, over low heat, until sugar dissolves. Stir in apple, apricot and half of the juice; bring to a boil. Reduce heat; simmer, uncovered, 2 minutes. Remove from heat; stir in remaining juice.
3 Spread fruit mixture over pastry sheet; roll into log. Cut log into quarters; place on prepared tray, 5cm apart, brush with remaining melted butter.
4 Bake, uncovered, in oven for about 20 minutes or until the scrolls are cooked through.
5 Meanwhile, combine yogurt, honey and remaining cinnamon in small bowl. Serve hot scrolls with spiced yogurt and dusted with sifted icing sugar, if desired.
PER SERVING *19.2g fat; 1442kJ (344 cal)*

SWEET BREADS

banana bread

preparation time 10 minutes cooking time 30 minutes makes 12 slices

1¼ cups (185g) self-raising flour

1 teaspoon ground cinnamon

20g butter

½ cup (100g) firmly packed brown sugar

1 egg, beaten lightly

¼ cup (60ml) milk

½ cup mashed banana

1 Preheat oven to 220°C/200°C fan-forced. Grease 14cm x 21cm loaf pan; line base with baking paper.

2 Sift flour and cinnamon into large bowl; rub in butter.

3 Stir in sugar, egg, milk and banana. Do not over-mix; the batter should be lumpy. Spoon mixture into prepared pan. Bake in oven about 30 minutes or until cooked when tested; cool.

4 Cut bread into 12 slices; toast lightly. Spread each with a tablespoon of cream cheese and drizzle with a teaspoon of honey, if desired.
PER SLICE *2.6g fat; 497kJ (119 cal)*

TIP Bread can be made a day ahead and is also suitable to freeze.

banana parkin

preparation time 20 minutes (plus standing time) cooking time 55 minutes makes 12 slices

You will need two large overripe bananas for this recipe.

125g butter

⅓ cup (75g) firmly packed brown sugar

⅔ cup (160ml) golden syrup

1⅓ cups (200g) plain flour

2 teaspoons bicarbonate soda

1 tablespoon ground ginger

¾ cup (65g) instant oats

1 egg, beaten lightly

1 cup mashed banana

1 Preheat oven to 180°C/160°C fan-forced. Grease deep 19cm square cake pan, line base with baking paper.

2 Combine butter, sugar and syrup in medium pan; stir over low heat until butter melts. Sift flour, soda and ginger into large bowl, add oats; stir in butter mixture, egg and banana. Pour mixture into prepared pan; bake in oven about 45 minutes. Stand parkin in pan 5 minutes; turn onto wire rack to cool. Serve sliced with butter, if desired.
PER SLICE *9.6g fat; 1078kJ (258 cal)*

STORE This can be made up to a week ahead. Keep stored in an airtight container.

honey almond bread

preparation time 35 minutes (plus cooling time) cooking time 45 minutes makes about 50

2 egg whites

¼ cup (55g) caster sugar

1 tablespoon honey

¾ cup (110g) plain flour

½ teaspoon mixed spice

½ cup (80g) almond kernels

1 Preheat oven to 180°C/160°C fan-forced. Grease 8cm x 26cm bar cake pan; line base and 2 long sides of pan with baking paper, extending paper 2cm above edge of pan.

2 Beat egg whites, sugar and honey in small bowl with electric mixer until sugar dissolves. Fold in sifted flour and spice, then nuts; spread mixture into prepared pan. Bake about 30 minutes or until browned lightly. Cool in pan, wrap in foil; stand overnight.

3 Preheat oven to 150°C/130°C fan-forced.

4 Using serrated knife, slice bread very thinly. Place slices on baking paper-lined oven trays; bake, uncovered, in oven about 15 minutes or until crisp.
PER PIECE *0.9g fat; 100kJ (24 cal)*

choc brownie muffins

preparation time 15 minutes cooking time 20 minutes makes 12

___

Take care not to overcook these little indulgences –
they should be slightly moist in the middle.

2 cups (300g) self-raising flour

⅓ cup (35g) cocoa powder

⅓ cup (75g) caster sugar

60g butter, melted

½ cup (95g) Choc Bits

½ cup (75g) pistachios, chopped coarsely

½ cup (165g) Nutella

1 egg, beaten lightly

¾ cup (180ml) milk

½ cup (120g) sour cream

1 Preheat oven to 200°C/180°C fan-forced. Grease 12-hole (⅓-cup/80ml) muffin pan.

2 Sift dry ingredients into large bowl; stir in remaining ingredients.

3 Divide mixture among holes of prepared pan.

4 Bake muffins in oven about 20 minutes. Stand muffins in pan for a few minutes before turning onto wire rack. Dust with sifted extra cocoa, if desired.
   PER MUFFIN 19.8g fat; 1530kJ (366 cal)

SWEET MUFFINS

banana maple muffins

preparation time 15 minutes cooking time 25 minutes makes 12

You will need about two small (260g) overripe bananas for this recipe.

2 cups (300g) self-raising flour

⅓ cup (50g) plain flour

½ teaspoon bicarbonate of soda

½ cup (110g) firmly packed brown sugar

¼ cup (60ml) maple-flavoured syrup

⅔ cup mashed banana

2 eggs, beaten lightly

1 cup (250ml) buttermilk

⅓ cup (80ml) vegetable oil

COCONUT TOPPING

15g butter

1 tablespoon maple-flavoured syrup

⅔ cup (30g) flaked coconut

1 Preheat oven to 200°C/180°C fan-forced. Grease 12-hole (⅓-cup/80ml) muffin pan.
2 Make coconut topping.
3 Sift dry ingredients into large bowl. Stir in syrup and banana, then egg, buttermilk and oil.
4 Divide mixture among holes of prepared pan; sprinkle mixture with coconut topping.
5 Bake muffins in oven about 20 minutes. Stand muffins in pan for a few minutes before turning onto wire rack.
   COCONUT TOPPING Melt butter in small saucepan, add syrup and coconut; stir constantly over high heat until coconut is browned lightly. Remove from heat.
   PER MUFFIN *10.5g fat; 1175kJ (281 cal)*

TIP Serve with crispy bacon for a scrumptious brunch with a difference.

ginger date muffins with caramel sauce

preparation time 15 minutes **cooking time** 35 minutes **makes** 12

1 cup (160g) seeded chopped dates

⅓ cup (80ml) water

¼ teaspoon bicarbonate of soda

2 cups (300g) self-raising flour

1 cup (150g) plain flour

2 teaspoons ground ginger

½ teaspoon mixed spice

1 cup (220g) firmly packed brown sugar

2 teaspoons grated orange rind

1 egg, beaten lightly

1¼ cups (310ml) milk

¼ cup (60ml) vegetable oil

CARAMEL SAUCE

1 cup (220g) firmly packed brown sugar

1 cup (250ml) cream

40g butter

1 Preheat oven to 200°C/180°C fan-forced. Grease 12-hole (⅓-cup/80ml) muffin pan.

2 Combine dates and water in small saucepan, bring to a boil; remove from heat, add soda, stand 5 minutes.

3 Meanwhile, sift dry ingredients into large bowl, stir in date mixture and remaining ingredients.

4 Divide mixture among holes of prepared pan.

5 Bake muffins in oven about 20 minutes. Stand muffins in pan for a few minutes before turning onto wire rack. Serve warm muffins drizzled with caramel sauce.

CARAMEL SAUCE Combine ingredients in medium saucepan. Stir over heat, without boiling, until sugar is dissolved, then simmer, without stirring, about 3 minutes or until thickened slightly.

PER SERVING *18.3g fat; 2040kJ (488 cal)*

TIP Fresh cream or a dollop of ice-cream makes this a delicious dessert.

day-before muffins

⅔ cup (100g) coarsely chopped dried apricots

½ cup (95g) coarsely chopped dried figs

1⅓ cups (95g) All-Bran breakfast cereal

1½ cups (375ml) skim milk

1¼ cups (250g) firmly packed brown sugar

1½ tablespoons golden syrup

1¼ cups (185g) self-raising flour

½ cup (60g) pecans, chopped coarsely

1 Combine apricot, fig, cereal, milk, sugar and syrup in large bowl; mix well. Cover; refrigerate overnight.

2 Preheat oven to 200°C/180°C fan-forced. Lightly grease four holes only of a six-hole texas ¾-cup (180ml) muffin pan.

3 Stir flour and nuts into apricot mixture. Spoon mixture into prepared muffin pan; bake in oven for 30 minutes. Serve muffins hot or cold. Dust with sifted icing sugar and top with dried apricots, if desired.
PER MUFFIN *11.1g fat; 2941kJ (704 cal)*

STORE Muffins can be frozen for up to two months.

orange and date dessert muffins

preparation time 10 minutes cooking time 20 minutes makes 12

2 cups (300g) self-raising flour

½ cup (75g) plain flour

½ teaspoon bicarbonate of soda

1¼ cups (250g) firmly packed brown sugar

125g butter, melted

1 cup (250ml) buttermilk

1 egg, beaten lightly

2 teaspoons finely grated orange rind

1 cup (160g) coarsely chopped dates

ORANGE SAUCE

¾ cup (150g) firmly packed brown sugar

2 teaspoons cornflour

⅓ cup (80ml) orange juice

2 tablespoons Grand Marnier

125g butter, chopped

1 tablespoon finely grated orange rind

1 Preheat oven to 200°C/180°C fan-forced. Grease and line 12-hole (⅓ cup/80ml) muffin pan with muffin cases.

2 Sift flours and soda into large bowl. Stir in sugar, then add butter, buttermilk, egg, rind and dates, stirring until just combined. Divide mixture among muffin cases.

3 Bake muffins, uncovered, in oven about 20 minutes. Stand 5 minutes. Serve muffins warm with orange sauce.
   ORANGE SAUCE Combine sugar and cornflour in small saucepan, gradually stir in juice and liqueur; bring to a boil, stirring until sauce boils and thickens. Stir in butter and rind.
   PER MUFFIN *18.4g fat; 1904kJ (455 cal)*

TIP Grand Marnier is an orange-flavoured liqueur based on cognac brandy.

basic muffins with apricots

preparation time 15 minutes (plus standing time) cooking time 20 minutes makes 12

1 cup (150g) coa rsely chopped dried apricots

3 cups (450g) self-raising flour

½ cup (110g) caster sugar

125g butter, chopped coarsely

½ cup (125ml) milk

2 eggs

1 Place apricot in small bowl; cover with boiling water. Cover; stand 30 minutes. Drain well.
2 Preheat oven to 200°C/180°C fan-forced.
3 Sift flour and sugar into large bowl; rub in butter using fingertips.
4 Add apricot to flour mixture.
5 Place milk and eggs in medium jug. Mix using fork; add to flour mixture. Mix using fork until ingredients are just combined; do not over-mix; mixture should be coarse and lumpy.
6 Divide mixture into greased 12-hole (⅓ cup/80ml) muffin pan. Bake in oven 20 minutes. Turn onto wire racks to cool. Serve with butter, if desired.
PER MUFFIN *10.3g fat; 1176kJ (281 cal)*

TIP Muffins are at their best freshly cooked and eaten warm with butter.
STORE Muffins can be stored in airtight container two days or frozen for up to two months.

wholemeal fig muffins

preparation time 10 minutes cooking time 20 minutes makes 12

2 cups (320g) wholemeal self-raising flour

1 cup (150g) self-raising flour

½ cup (110g) raw sugar

125g butter, chopped coarsely

1 cup (190g) coarsely chopped dried figs

2 eggs, beaten lightly

1 cup (250ml) milk

1 Preheat oven to 200°C/180 °C fan-forced.
2 Place flours in large bowl. Add sugar; rub in butter.
3 Add figs, then combined egg and milk. Mix using fork until ingredients are just combined; do not over-mix. Mixture should be coarse and lumpy.
4 Divide mixture into greased 12-hole (⅓ cup/80ml) muffin pan. Bake in oven 20 minutes. Turn onto wire racks to cool. Serve with butter and a drizzle of honey, if desired.
PER MUFFIN *11.1g fat; 1258kJ (301 cal)*

STORE Muffins can be stored in airtight container two days or frozen for up to two months.

raspberry and coconut muffins

preparation time 10 minutes cooking time 20 minutes makes 12

2½ cups (375g) self-raising flour

90g butter, chopped

1 cup (220g) caster sugar

1¼ cups (310ml) buttermilk

1 egg, beaten lightly

⅓ cup (30g) desiccated coconut

150g fresh or frozen raspberries

2 tablespoons shredded coconut

1 Preheat oven to 200°C/180°C fan-forced. Grease 12-hole (⅓-cup/80ml) muffin pan.

2 Place flour in large bowl; using fingertips, rub in butter. Add caster sugar, buttermilk, egg, desiccated coconut and raspberries; mix until just combined.

3 Divide mixture among holes of prepared pan; sprinkle mixture with shredded coconut.

4 Bake muffins in oven about 20 minutes. Stand muffins in pan for a few minutes before turning onto wire rack.
   PER MUFFIN *9.8g fat; 1195kJ (286 cal)*

TIP Two kinds of coconut – finely grated in the mix and shredded on top – create a moist morsel with a contrasting crunch.

apple and custard muffins

preparation time 20 minutes cooking time 25 minutes makes 12

90g butter, melted

2 cups (300g) self-raising flour

1 cup (150g) plain flour

½ teaspoon ground cinnamon

¾ cup (165g) caster sugar

1 egg, beaten lightly

1 cup (250ml) milk

¼ cup (60ml) packaged thick custard

½ cup (110g) canned pie apples

2 tablespoons brown sugar

½ teaspoon ground cinnamon, extra

1 Preheat oven to 200°C/180°C fan-forced. Grease 12-hole (⅓-cup/80ml) muffin pan, or line with paper patty cases.

2 Combine butter, flours, cinnamon, caster sugar, egg and milk in large bowl; stir until just combined.

3 Divide half the mixture among holes of prepared pan; make well in centre of each muffin, drop 1 level teaspoon of custard and 2 level teaspoons of apple into each well. Top with remaining muffin mixture; sprinkle with combined brown sugar and extra cinnamon.

4 Bake muffins in oven about 25 minutes. Stand muffins in pan for a few minutes before turning onto wire rack.
   PER MUFFIN *7.5g fat; 1137kJ (272 cal)*

TIP A crumbly topping hides the custard and apple surprise.

honey, sultana and pecan muffins

preparation time 10 minutes cooking time 25 minutes makes 12

You will need about two small (260g) overripe bananas for this recipe.

2 cups (300g) self-raising flour

2 teaspoons ground cinnamon

¾ cup (150g) firmly packed brown sugar

½ cup (50g) chopped pecans

½ cup (80g) sultanas

¼ cup (90g) honey

¾ cup mashed banana

¼ cup (70g) low-fat yoghurt

¾ cup (180ml) low-fat milk

2 eggs, beaten lightly

1 Preheat oven to 200°C/180°C fan-forced. Grease 12-hole (⅓-cup/80ml) muffin pan.

2 Sift flour and cinnamon into large bowl. Add sugar, nuts and sultanas, then combined remaining ingredients. Stir until ingredients just combined.

3 Divide mixture among holes of prepared pan.

4 Bake muffins in oven about 25 minutes. Stand muffins in pan for a few minutes before turning onto wire rack. Dust with sifted icing sugar and top with a light sprinkling of cinnamon, if desired.
PER MUFFIN *4.2g fat; 1028kJ (246 cal)*

TIP Low in fat, big on flavour, these moist muffins are perfect for a picnic.

citrus poppy seed muffins

preparation time 15 minutes cooking time 20 minutes makes 12

125g softened butter, chopped

2 teaspoons finely grated lemon rind

2 teaspoons finely grated lime rind

2 teaspoons finely grated orange rind

⅔ cup (150g) caster sugar

2 eggs, beaten lightly

2 cups (300g) self-raising flour

½ cup (125ml) milk

2 tablespoons poppy seeds

1 medium orange (240g)

icing sugar, for dusting

1 Preheat oven to 200°C/180°C fan-forced. Grease 12-hole (⅓-cup/80ml) muffin pan.

2 Combine butter, rinds, caster sugar, egg, sifted flour and milk in medium bowl; beat with electric mixer until just combined. Increase speed to medium; beat until mixture is just changed in colour; stir in poppy seeds.

3 Divide mixture among holes of prepared pan.

4 Bake muffins in oven about 20 minutes. Stand muffins in pan for a few minutes before turning onto wire rack.

5 Peel rind thinly from orange, avoiding any white pith. Cut rind into thin strips. To serve, dust muffins with icing sugar; top with orange strips.
PER MUFFIN *11g fat; 1037kJ (248 cal)*

TIP The tiny, blue-grey poppy seeds add texture and a slightly nutty taste.

marmalade almond muffins

preparation time 15 minutes cooking time 20 minutes makes 12

2 cups (300g) self-raising flour

125g butter, chopped

1 cup (80g) flaked almonds

⅔ cup (150g) caster sugar

1 tablespoon finely grated orange rind

½ cup (170g) orange marmalade

2 eggs, beaten lightly

½ cup (125ml) milk

¼ cup (20g) flaked almonds, extra

ORANGE SYRUP

¼ cup (85g) orange marmalade

2 tablespoons water

1 Preheat oven to 200°C/180°C fan-forced. Grease 12-hole (⅓-cup/80ml) muffin pan.
2 Sift flour into large bowl, rub in butter. Stir in nuts, sugar and rind, then marmalade, egg and milk.
3 Divide mixture among holes of prepared pan; sprinkle with extra nuts.
4 Bake muffins in oven about 20 minutes. Stand muffins in pan for a few minutes before turning onto wire rack. Serve warm muffins drizzled with orange syrup.
   ORANGE SYRUP Combine ingredients in a small bowl.
   PER SERVING *14.8g fat; 1425kJ (341 cal)*

mixed berry buttermilk muffins

preparation time 5 minutes cooking time 20 minutes (plus standing time) makes 12

We used 50g frozen blueberries, 50g frozen blackberries and 100g frozen raspberries in this recipe.

2½ cups (375g) self-raising flour

¾ cup (165g) caster sugar

1 egg, beaten lightly

1 teaspoon vanilla extract

⅔ cup (160ml) vegetable oil

¾ cup (180ml) buttermilk

200g frozen mixed berries

1 Preheat oven to 200°C/180°C fan-forced. Line 12-hole ⅓-cup (80ml) muffin pan with paper cases or grease holes of pan.
2 Sift flour and sugar into large bowl; stir in remaining ingredients.
3 Divide mixture muffin among holes of prepared pan; bake in oven about 20 minutes. Stand 5 minutes; turn onto wire rack, turn muffins top-side up to cool.
   PER MUFFIN *13.4g fat; 1192kJ (285 cal)*

TIPS Be careful not to over-mix muffin mixture; it should be slightly lumpy. Use still-frozen berries to minimise "bleeding" of colour into the mixture.
STORE These muffins freeze well; wrap them individually in plastic wrap so you only need to defrost a certain number of them at any time.

mixed berry muffins

preparation time 10 minutes cooking time 35 minutes makes 6

2¼ cups (335g) self-raising flour

1 cup (220g) caster sugar

1 teaspoon vanilla extract

2 eggs, beaten lightly

100g butter, melted

1 cup (250ml) milk

1 teaspoon grated lemon rind

200g fresh or frozen mixed berries

1 Preheat oven to 200°C/180°C fan-forced. Grease six-hole (¾-cup/180ml) texas muffin pan or spray six large disposable muffin cases and place on an oven tray.

2 Sift flour into large bowl; add sugar then combined extract, egg, butter, milk and rind. Add berries; stir through gently.

3 Divide muffin mixture among holes of prepared pans.

4 Bake muffins in oven about 35 minutes. Stand muffins in pan for a few minutes before turning onto wire rack.
PER MUFFIN *17.8g fat; 2190kJ (524 cal)*

TIP Taste-test combinations when berries are in season and freeze your favourites.

overnight date and muesli muffins

preparation time 10 minutes (plus refrigeration time) cooking time 20 minutes makes 12

1¼ cups (185g) plain flour

1¼ cups (160g) toasted muesli

1 teaspoon ground cinnamon

1 teaspoon bicarbonate of soda

½ cup (110g) firmly packed brown sugar

½ cup (30g) unprocessed bran

¾ cup (120g) coarsely chopped dates

1½ cups (375ml) buttermilk

½ cup (125ml) vegetable oil

1 egg, beaten lightly

1 Combine ingredients in large bowl, stir until just combined. Cover, refrigerate overnight.

2 Preheat oven to 200°C/180°C fan-forced. Grease 12-hole (⅓-cup/80ml) muffin pan.

3 Divide mixture among holes of prepared pan.

4 Bake muffins in oven about 20 minutes. Stand muffins in pan for a few minutes before turning onto wire rack.
PER SERVING *12.7g fat; 1212kJ (290 cal)*

TIP A filling, classic, healthy muffin that is simple to prepare.

white chocolate and macadamia muffins

preparation time 10 minutes cooking time 20 minutes makes 6

2 cups (300g) self-raising flour

⅔ cup (150g) caster sugar

¾ cup (140g) white Choc Bits

½ cup (75g) coarsely chopped macadamias, toasted

60g butter, melted

¾ cup (180ml) milk

1 egg, beaten lightly

1 Preheat oven to 200°C/180°C fan-forced. Grease six-hole (¾-cup/180ml) texas muffin pan.

2 Sift flour and sugar into large bowl; stir in remaining ingredients. Divide mixture among holes of prepared pan.

3 Bake muffins in oven about 20 minutes. Stand muffins in pan for a few minutes before turning onto wire rack.
   PER MUFFIN *28.2g fat; 2504kJ (599 cal)*

gluten-free, dairy-free raspberry muffins

preparation time 15 minutes cooking time 20 minutes makes 12

2½ cups (375g) gluten-free plain flour

1 tablespoon gluten-free baking powder

½ teaspoon bicarbonate of soda

⅓ cup (40g) rice bran

⅔ cup (150g) firmly packed brown sugar

1½ cups (375ml) soy milk

1 teaspoon vanilla extract

60g dairy-free spread, melted

2 eggs, beaten lightly

150g frozen raspberries

1 tablespoon coffee crystals

1 Preheat oven to 200°C/180°C fan-forced. Grease 12-hole (⅓-cup/80ml) muffin pan, or line with paper patty cases.

2 Sift flour, baking powder and soda into large bowl. Stir in bran, sugar, combined milk, extract, spread and egg until almost combined. Add raspberries, stir until just combined.

3 Divide mixture among holes of prepared pan; sprinkle with coffee crystals.

4 Bake in oven about 20 minutes. Stand muffins in pan for a few minutes before carefully removing from pan to cool on wire rack.
   PER SERVING *6.7g fat; 1062kJ (254 cal)*

   TIP These muffins are a fabulous choice for people with allergies.

basic scones

preparation time 20 minutes cooking time 15 minutes makes 16

Scones served hot from the oven with butter or jam and cream are delightful for morning or afternoon tea. There's no mystery to making light, fluffy scones; just follow our instructions.

2½ cups (375g) self-raising flour

1 tablespoon caster sugar

¼ teaspoon salt

30g butter

¾ cup (180ml) milk

½ cup (125ml) water, approximately

1 Preheat oven to 240°C/220°C fan-forced. Grease deep 19cm square cake pan.
2 Sift flour, sugar and salt into large bowl; rub in butter with fingertips.
3 Make well in centre of flour mixture; add milk and almost all of the water. Using a knife, "cut" the milk and water through the flour mixture to mix to a soft, sticky dough. Add remaining water only if needed for correct consistency.
4 Turn dough onto lightly floured surface; knead quickly and lightly until smooth.
5 Use hand to press dough out evenly to 2cm thickness.
6 Dip 4.5cm cutter into flour; cut as many rounds as you can from the piece of dough. Place scones side by side, just touching, in prepared pan. Gently knead scraps of dough together, and repeat pressing and cutting out of dough. Place rounds in prepared pan; brush tops with a little extra milk.
7 Bake scones in oven about 15 minutes.
PER SCONE *2.3g fat; 477kJ (107 cal)*

SWEET SCONES

sultana and lemon scones

preparation time 25 minutes cooking time 15 minutes makes 16

2½ cups (375g) self-raising flour

1 tablespoon caster sugar

¼ teaspoon salt

30g butter

½ cup (80g) sultanas

2 teaspoons grated lemon rind

¾ cup (180ml) milk

½ cup (125ml) water, approximately

1 Preheat oven to 240°C/220°C fan-forced. Grease deep 19cm square cake pan.
2 Sift flour, sugar and salt into large bowl; rub in butter with fingertips. Stir in sultanas and rind.
3 Make well in centre of flour mixture; add milk and almost all of the water. Using a knife, "cut" the milk and water through the flour mixture to mix to a soft, sticky dough. Add remaining water only if needed for correct consistency.
4 Turn dough onto lightly floured surface; knead quickly and lightly until smooth.
5 Use hand to press dough out evenly to 2cm thickness.
6 Dip 4.5cm cutter into flour; cut as many rounds as you can from the piece of dough. Place scones side by side, just touching, in prepared pan. Gently knead scraps of dough together, and repeat pressing and cutting out of dough. Place rounds in prepared pan; brush tops with a little extra milk.
7 Bake scones in oven about 15 minutes. Serve with jam, if desired.
   PER SCONE 2.8g fat; 518kJ (124 cal)

cardamom marmalade scones

preparation time 25 minutes cooking time 15 minutes makes 16

2½ cups (375g) self-raising flour

1 tablespoon caster sugar

¼ teaspoon salt

30g butter

1 teaspoon ground cardamom

2 teaspoons grated orange rind

1 cup (250ml) milk

⅓ cup (115g) orange marmalade

1 Preheat oven to 240°C/220°C fan-forced. Grease deep 19cm square cake pan.
2 Sift flour, sugar and salt into large bowl; rub in butter with fingertips. Stir in cardamom and rind.
3 Make well in centre of flour mixture; add milk and marmalade. Using a knife, "cut" the milk and marmalade through the flour mixture to mix to a soft, sticky dough.
4 Turn dough onto lightly floured surface; knead quickly and lightly until smooth.
5 Use hand to press dough out evenly to 2cm thickness.
6 Dip 4.5cm cutter into flour; cut as many rounds as you can from the piece of dough. Place scones side by side, just touching, in prepared pan. Gently knead scraps of dough together, and repeat pressing and cutting out of dough. Place rounds in prepared pan; brush tops with a little extra milk.
7 Bake scones in oven about 15 minutes. Serve with cream, if desired.
   PER SCONE 2.4g fat; 535kJ (128 cal)

blueberry ginger scones

preparation time 25 minutes cooking time 15 minutes makes 16

2½ cups (375g) self-raising flour

1 tablespoon caster sugar

¼ teaspoon salt

30g butter

3 teaspoons ground ginger

½ cup (75g) fresh or frozen blueberries

¾ cup (180ml) milk

½ cup (125ml) water, approximately

1 Preheat oven to 240°C/220°C fan-forced. Grease deep 19cm square cake pan.
2 Sift flour, sugar and salt into large bowl; rub in butter with fingertips. Stir in ground ginger and blueberries.
3 Make well in centre of flour mixture; add milk and almost all of the water. Using a knife, "cut" the milk and water through the flour mixture to mix to a soft, sticky dough. Add remaining water only if needed for correct consistency.
4 Turn dough onto lightly floured surface; knead quickly and lightly until smooth.
5 Use hand to press dough out evenly to 2cm thickness.
6 Dip 4.5cm cutter into flour; cut as many rounds as you can from the piece of dough. Place scones side by side, just touching, in prepared pan. Gently knead scraps of dough together, and repeat pressing and cutting out of dough. Place rounds in prepared pan; brush tops with a little extra milk.
7 Bake scones in oven about 15 minutes.
   PER SCONE *2.3g fat; 456kJ (109 cal)*

buttermilk scones

preparation time 20 minutes cooking time 15 minutes makes 16

2½ cups (375g) self-raising flour

1 tablespoon caster sugar

¼ teaspoon salt

30g butter

1¼ cups (310ml) buttermilk, approximately

1 Preheat oven to 240°C/220°C fan-forced. Grease deep 19cm-square cake pan.
2 Sift flour, sugar and salt into large bowl; rub in butter with fingertips.
3 Make well in centre of flour mixture; add buttermilk. Using a knife, "cut" the buttermilk through the flour mixture to mix to a soft, sticky dough.
4 Turn dough onto lightly floured surface; knead quickly and lightly until smooth.
5 Use hand to press dough out evenly to 2cm thickness.
6 Dip 4.5cm cutter into flour; cut as many rounds as you can from the piece of dough. Place scones side by side, just touching, in prepared pan. Gently knead scraps of dough together, and repeat pressing and cutting out of dough. Place rounds in prepared pan; brush tops with a little milk.
7 Bake scones in oven about 15 minutes. Serve with jam, if desired.
   PER SCONE *2.2g fat; 460kJ (110 cal)*

honey and muesli scones

preparation time 25 minutes cooking time 15 minutes makes 16

2½ cups (375g) self-raising flour

1 tablespoon caster sugar

¼ teaspoon salt

30g butter

1 teaspoon ground cinnamon

½ cup (65g) toasted muesli

¼ cup (90g) honey

¾ cup (180ml) milk

1 Preheat oven to 240°C/220°C fan-forced. Grease deep 19cm square cake pan.
2 Sift flour, sugar and salt into large bowl; rub in butter with fingertips. Stir in cinnamon and toasted muesli.
3 Make well in centre of flour mixture; add honey, and then milk. Using a knife, "cut" the honey and milk through the flour mixture to mix to a soft, sticky dough.
4 Turn dough onto lightly floured surface; knead quickly and lightly until smooth.
5 Use hand to press dough out evenly to 2cm thickness.
6 Dip 4.5cm cutter into flour; cut as many rounds as you can from the piece of dough. Place scones side by side, just touching, in prepared pan. Gently knead scraps of dough together, and repeat pressing and cutting out of dough. Place rounds in prepared pan; brush tops with a little extra milk.
7 Bake scones in oven about 15 minutes. Serve with butter, if desired.
   PER SCONE *2.8g fat; 585kJ (140 cal)*

apricot and almond scones

preparation time 25 minutes cooking time 15 minutes makes 16

2½ cups (375g) self-raising flour

1 tablespoon caster sugar

¼ teaspoon salt

30g butter

1 teaspoon mixed spice

1 cup (150g) chopped dried apricots

⅓ cup (45g) chopped toasted slivered almonds

¾ cup (180ml) milk

½ cup (125ml) water, approximately

1 Preheat oven to 240°C/220°C fan-forced. Grease deep 19cm-square cake pan.
2 Sift flour, sugar and salt into large bowl; rub in butter with fingertips. Stir in mixed spice, apricot and nuts.
3 Make well in centre of flour mixture; add milk and almost all of the water. Using a knife, "cut" the milk and water through the flour mixture to mix to a soft, sticky dough. Add remaining water only if needed for correct consistency.
4 Turn dough onto lightly floured surface; knead quickly and lightly until smooth.
5 Use hand to press dough out evenly to 2cm thickness.
6 Dip 4.5cm cutter into flour; cut as many rounds as you can from the piece of dough. Place scones side by side, just touching, in prepared pan. Gently knead scraps of dough together, and repeat pressing and cutting out of dough. Place rounds in prepared pan; brush tops with a little extra milk.
7 Bake scones in oven about 15 minutes. Serve with cream, if desired.
   PER SCONE *3.8g fat; 598kJ (143 cal)*

ALMONDS flat, pointy-tipped nuts having a pitted brown shell enclosing a creamy white kernel which is covered by a brown skin.
flaked paper-thin slices.
slivered small pieces cut lengthways.

ARROWROOT a starch used mostly as a thickening agent. Cornflour can be substituted but does not make as clear a glaze and imparts its own taste.

ARTICHOKE HEARTS tender centre of the globe artichoke; can be harvested from the plant after the prickly choke is removed. Buy from delicatessens or canned in brine.

BALSAMIC VINEGAR originally from Modena, Italy, there are now many balsamic vinegars on the market ranging in pungency and quality depending on how, and for how long, they have been aged. Quality can be determined up to a point by price; use the most expensive sparingly.

BICARBONATE OF SODA also known as baking soda.

BLACK MUSTARD SEEDS also known as brown mustard seeds; more pungent than the white variety; used frequently in curries.

BLACK POPPY SEEDS small, dried, bluish-grey seeds of the poppy plant, with a crunchy texture and a nutty flavour. Can be purchased whole or ground.

BRIOCHE French in origin; a rich, yeast-leavened, cake-like bread made with butter and eggs. Eaten freshly baked or toasted; available from cake or specialty bread shops.

CAPERS the grey-green buds of a warm climate shrub, sold either dried and salted or pickled in a vinegar brine. Their pungent taste adds piquancy to a classic steak tartare, tapenade, sauces and condiments.

CAPSICUM also known as pepper or bell pepper. Seeds and membranes should be discarded before use.

CAYENNE also known as cayenne pepper; a thin-fleshed, long, extremely hot, dried red chilli, usually purchased ground.

CHEESE
brie soft-ripened cow-milk cheese with a delicate, creamy texture and a rich, sweet taste that varies from buttery to mushroomy.

cheddar the most common cow-milk tasty cheese; should be aged, hard and have a pronounced bite.
fetta Greek in origin; a crumbly textured goat- or sheep-milk cheese having a sharp, salty taste. Ripened and stored in salted whey; particularly good cubed and tossed into salads.
fontina a firm Italian cow-milk cheese with a creamy, nutty taste and brown or red rind; an ideal melting or grilling cheese.
mascarpone an Italian fresh cultured-cream product made in much the same way as yogurt. It is used in many Italian desserts and as an accompaniment to fresh fruit.
mozzarella soft, spun-curd cheese. Generally manufactured from cow milk, it is the most popular pizza cheese because of its low melting point and elasticity when heated (used for texture rather than flavour).
parmesan also known as parmigiano; a hard, grainy cow-milk cheese; grated or flaked and used for pasta, salads and soups; it is also eaten on its own with fruit.
ricotta a soft, sweet, moist, white cow-milk cheese with a low fat content (about 8.5 per cent) and a slightly grainy texture.

CHOC BITS also known as chocolate chips or chocolate morsels; available in milk, white and dark chocolate. Made of cocoa liquor, cocoa butter, sugar and an emulsifier, these hold their shape in baking.

CIABATTA in Italian, the word means slipper, the traditional shape of this popular crisp-crusted, open-textured white sourdough bread. A good bread to use for bruschetta.

COCONUT
desiccated concentrated, dried, unsweetened, finely shredded coconut flesh.
flaked dried flaked coconut flesh.
shredded unsweetened thin strips of dried coconut flesh.

CORIANDER also known as cilantro, pak chee or chinese parsley; bright-green-leafed herb having both pungent aroma and taste. Coriander seeds are dried and sold either whole or ground, and neither form tastes remotely like the fresh leaf but rather like an acrid combination of sage and caraway.

CORNFLOUR also known as cornstarch. Available made from corn or wheat (wheaten cornflour, gluten-free, gives a lighter texture in cakes); used as a thickening agent in cooking.

CUMIN also known as zeera or comino; resembling caraway in size, cumin is the dried seed of a plant related to the parsley family. Available dried as seeds or ground. Black cumin seeds are smaller than standard cumin, and dark brown rather than true black; they are mistakenly confused with kalonji.

DATES fruit of the date palm tree, eaten fresh or dried, on their own or in prepared dishes. About 4cm to 6cm in length, oval and plump, thin-skinned, with a honey-sweet flavour and sticky texture. Best known, perhaps, for its inclusion in sticky toffee pudding; also found in muesli and other cereals; muffins, scones and cakes; compotes and stewed fruit desserts.

DHAL an Indian food term used to describe both a whole spectrum of lentils, dried peas and beans, and the range of spicy stew-like dishes containing them.

FLOUR
besan also known as chickpea flour or gram; made from ground chickpeas so is gluten-free and high in protein. Used in Indian cooking to make dumplings, noodles and chapati; for a batter coating for deep-frying; and as a sauce thickener.
plain also known as all-purpose; unbleached wheat flour is the best for baking: the gluten content ensures a strong dough, which produces a light result. Also used as a thickening agent in sauces and gravies.
self-raising all-purpose plain or wholemeal flour with baking powder and salt added; can be made at home with plain or wholemeal flour sifted with baking powder in the proportion of 1 cup flour to 2 teaspoons baking powder.
wholemeal also known as wholewheat flour; milled with the wheat germ so is higher in fibre and more nutritional than plain flour.

GLOSSARY

GARAM MASALA literally meaning blended spices in its northern Indian place of origin; based on varying proportions of cardamom, cinnamon, cloves, coriander, fennel and cumin, roasted and ground together. Black pepper and chilli can be added for a hotter version.

GELATINE we use powdered gelatine in the recipes in this book; it's also available in sheet form known as leaf gelatine; a thickening agent. Two teaspoons of powdered gelatine (7g or one sachet) is roughly equivalent to four gelatine leaves. The two types are interchangable but leaf gelatine gives a much clearer mixture than powdered gelatine; it's perfect in dishes where appearance really counts.

GHEE clarified butter; with the milk solids removed, this fat has a high smoking point so can be heated to a high temperature without burning.

GREEN ONIONS also known as scallion or (incorrectly) shallot; an immature onion picked before the bulb has formed, having a long, bright-green edible stalk.

KALONJI also known as nigella or black onion seeds. Tiny, angular seeds, black on the outside and creamy within, with a sharp nutty flavour that can be enhanced by frying briefly in a dry hot pan before use; can be found in most Asian and Middle Eastern food shops. Often erroneously called black cumin seeds.

MARMALADE a preserve, usually based on citrus fruit and its rind, cooked with sugar until the mixture has an intense flavour and thick consistency. Orange, lemon and lime are some of the commercially prepared varieties available.

MILK we use full-cream homogenised milk unless otherwise specified.
buttermilk in spite of its name, buttermilk is actually low in fat, varying between 0.6 per cent and 2.0 per cent per 100 ml; is intentionally made from no-fat or low-fat milk to which specific bacterial cultures have been added during the manufacturing process. A good substitute for dairy products such as cream or sour cream in some baking and salad dressings.
skim sometimes labelled no-fat; both have 0.1 per cent fat content.

MIXED SPICE a classic mixture generally containing caraway, allspice, coriander, cumin, nutmeg and ginger, although cinnamon and other spices can be added. It is used with fruit and in cakes.

MUSHROOMS
button small, cultivated white mushrooms with a mild flavour. When a recipe in this book calls for an unspecified type of mushroom, use button.
flat large, flat mushrooms with a rich earthy flavour, ideal for filling and barbecuing. They are sometimes misnamed field mushrooms, which are wild mushrooms.

NECTARINES smooth-skinned, slightly smaller cousin to the peach; juicy, with a rich and rather spicy flavour. Good for desserts peeled and sliced with a little cinnamon sugar and lemon.

NEW POTATOES also known as chats; not a separate variety but an early harvest with very thin skin.

NUTMEG a strong and very pungent spice ground from the dried nut of an evergreen tree native to Indonesia. Usually found ground but the flavour is more intense from a whole nut, available from spice shops, so it's best to grate your own. Used most often in baking and milk-based desserts and sauces, but also works nicely in savoury dishes. Found in mixed spice mixtures.

PAPRIKA ground dried sweet red capsicum (bell pepper); there are many grades and types available, including sweet, hot, mild and smoked.

PEANUT OIL an oil pressed from ground peanuts; the most commonly used oil in Asian cooking because of its high smoke point (capacity to handle high heat without burning).

PECANS native to the US and now grown locally; pecans are golden brown, buttery and rich. Good in savoury as well as sweet dishes; walnuts are a good substitute.

PESTO a classic uncooked sauce made from basil, garlic, parmesan and olive oil; often served over pasta.

PINE NUTS also known as pignoli; not in fact a nut but a small, cream-coloured kernel from pine cones. They are best roasted before use to bring out the flavour.

PISTACHIO green, delicately flavoured nuts inside hard off-white shells. Available salted or unsalted in their shells; you can also get them shelled.

POLENTA also known as cornmeal; a flour-like cereal made of dried corn (maize). also the name of the dish made from it.

PROSCIUTTO a kind of unsmoked Italian ham; salted, air-cured and aged, it is usually eaten uncooked.

RAISINS dried sweet grapes.

ROCKET also known as arugula, rugula and rucola; peppery green leaf eaten raw in salads or used in cooking. Baby rocket leaves are smaller and less peppery.

SAMBAL OELEK also ulek or olek; Indonesian in origin, this is a salty paste made from ground chillies and vinegar.

SUGAR we use coarse, granulated table sugar, also known as crystal sugar, unless otherwise specified.
brown an extremely soft, fine granulated sugar retaining molasses for its characteristic colour and flavour.
caster also known as superfine or finely granulated table sugar. The fine crystals dissolve easily so it is perfect for cakes, meringues and desserts.
demerara small-grained golden-coloured crystal sugar.
icing also known as confectioners' sugar or powdered sugar; pulverised granulated sugar crushed together with a small amount (about 3 per cent) of cornflour.

TREACLE thick, dark syrup not unlike molasses.

TURMERIC also known as kamin; is a rhizome related to galangal and ginger. Must be grated or pounded to release its somewhat acrid aroma and pungent flavour. Known for the golden colour it imparts, fresh turmeric can be substituted with the more common dried powder.

WHOLEGRAIN MUSTARD also known as seeded. A French-style coarse-grain mustard made from crushed mustard seeds and dijon-style french mustard. Works well with cold meats and sausages.

YEAST (dried and fresh), a raising agent used in dough making. A microscopic living organism that grows best in warm, moist conditions; over-hot conditions or dissolving liquid will kill yeast and keep the dough from rising. Granular (7g sachets) and fresh compressed (20g pieces) yeast can almost always be substituted one for the other when yeast is called for in a recipe.

ZUCCHINI also known as courgette; small, pale- or dark-green, yellow or white vegetable belonging to the squash family. Harvested when young, its edible flowers can be stuffed with a mild cheese or other similarly delicate ingredients then deep-fried or oven-baked to make a delicious appetiser. Good cored and stuffed with various meat or rice fillings; and in Italian vegetable dishes and pasta sauces.

MEASURES

One Australian metric measuring cup holds approximately 250ml; one Australian metric tablespoon holds 20ml; one Australian metric teaspoon holds 5ml.

The difference between one country's measuring cups and another's is within a two- or three-teaspoon variance, and will not affect your cooking results. North America, New Zealand and the United Kingdom use a 15ml tablespoon.

All cup and spoon measurements are level. The most accurate way of measuring dry ingredients is to weigh them. When measuring liquids, use a clear glass or plastic jug with the metric markings.

We use large eggs with an average weight of 60g.

DRY MEASURES

METRIC	IMPERIAL
15g	½oz
30g	1oz
60g	2oz
90g	3oz
125g	4oz (¼lb)
155g	5oz
185g	6oz
220g	7oz
250g	8oz (½lb)
280g	9oz
315g	10oz
345g	11oz
375g	12oz (¾lb)
410g	13oz
440g	14oz
470g	15oz
500g	16oz (1lb)
750g	24oz (1½lb)
1kg	32oz (2lb)

LIQUID MEASURES

METRIC	IMPERIAL
30ml	1 fluid oz
60ml	2 fluid oz
100ml	3 fluid oz
125ml	4 fluid oz
150ml	5 fluid oz (¼ pint/1 gill)
190ml	6 fluid oz
250ml	8 fluid oz
300ml	10 fluid oz (½ pint)
500ml	16 fluid oz
600ml	20 fluid oz (1 pint)
1000ml (1 litre)	1¾ pints

LENGTH MEASURES

METRIC	IMPERIAL
3mm	⅛in
6mm	¼in
1cm	½in
2cm	¾in
2.5cm	1in
5cm	2in
6cm	2½in
8cm	3in
10cm	4in
13cm	5in
15cm	6in
18cm	7in
20cm	8in
23cm	9in
25cm	10in
28cm	11in
30cm	12in (1ft)

OVEN TEMPERATURES

These oven temperatures are only a guide for conventional ovens. For fan-forced ovens, check the manufacturer's manual.

	°C (CELSIUS)	°F (FAHRENHEIT)	GAS MARK
Very slow	120	250	½
Slow	150	275-300	1-2
Moderately slow	160	325	3
Moderate	180	350-375	4-5
Moderately hot	200	400	6
Hot	220	425-450	7-8
Very hot	240	475	9

CONVERSION CHART

ARE YOU MISSING SOME OF THE WORLD'S FAVOURITE COOKBOOKS?

The Australian Women's Weekly Cookbooks are available from bookshops, cookshops, supermarkets and other stores all over the world. You can also buy direct from the publisher, using the order form below.

ACP Magazines Ltd Privacy Notice
This book may contain offers, competitions or surveys that require you to provide information about yourself if you choose to enter or take part in any such Reader Offer. If you provide information about yourself to ACP Magazines Ltd, the company will use this information to provide you with the products or services you have requested, and may supply your information to contractors that help ACP to do this. ACP will also use your information to inform you of other ACP publications, products, services and events. ACP will also give your information to organisations that are providing special prizes or offers, and that are clearly associated with the Reader Offer. Unless you tell us not to, we may give your information to other organisations that use it to inform you about other products, services and events or who may give it to other organisations that may use it for this purpose. If you would like to gain access to the information ACP holds about you, please contact ACP's Privacy Officer at ACP Magazines Ltd, 54-58 Park Street, Sydney, NSW 2000, Australia.

☐ **Privacy Notice** Please do not provide information about me to any organisation not associated with this offer.

To order: Mail or fax – photocopy or complete the order form above, and send your credit card details or cheque payable to: Australian Consolidated Press (UK), ACP Books, 10 Scirocco Close, Moulton Park Office Village, Northampton NN3 6AP
phone (+44) (0)1604 642200
fax (+44) (0)1604 642300
email books@acpuk.com
or order online at www.acpuk.com
Non-UK residents: We accept the credit cards listed on the coupon, or cheques, drafts or International Money Orders payable in sterling and drawn on a UK bank. Credit card charges are at the exchange rate current at the time of payment.
Postage and packing UK: Add £1.00 per order plus £1.75 per book.
Postage and packing overseas: Add £2.00 per order plus £3.50 per book. All pricing current at time of going to press and subject to change/availability.
Offer ends 31.12.2008

TITLE	RRP	QTY	TITLE	RRP	QTY
100 Fast Fillets	£6.99		Indian Cooking Class	£6.99	
After Work Fast	£6.99		Japanese Cooking Class	£6.99	
Beginners Cooking Class	£6.99		Just For One	£6.99	
Beginners Thai	£6.99		Just For Two	£6.99	
Best Food Desserts	£6.99		Kids' Birthday Cakes	£6.99	
Best Food Fast	£6.99		Kids Cooking	£6.99	
Breads & Muffins	£6.99		Kids' Cooking Step-by-Step	£6.99	
Cafe Classics	£6.99		Low-carb, Low-fat	£6.99	
Cakes Bakes & Desserts	£6.99		Low-fat Feasts	£6.99	
Cakes Biscuits & Slices	£6.99		Low-fat Food for Life	£6.99	
Cakes Cooking Class	£6.99		Low-fat Meals in Minutes	£6.99	
Caribbean Cooking	£6.99		Main Course Salads	£6.99	
Casseroles	£6.99		Mexican	£6.99	
Casseroles & Slow-Cooked Classics	£6.99		Middle Eastern Cooking Class	£6.99	
Cheap Eats	£6.99		Mince in Minutes	£6.99	
Cheesecakes: baked and chilled	£6.99		Moroccan & the Foods of North Africa	£6.99	
Chicken	£6.99		Muffins, Scones & Breads	£6.99	
Chicken Meals in Minutes	£6.99		New Casseroles	£6.99	
Chinese & the foods of Thailand, Vietnam, Malaysia & Japan	£6.99		New Curries	£6.99	
			New Finger Food	£6.99	
Chinese Cooking Class	£6.99		New French Food	£6.99	
Christmas Cooking	£6.99		New Salads	£6.99	
Chocolate	£6.99		Party Food and Drink	£6.99	
Chocs & Treats	£6.99		Pasta Meals in Minutes	£6.99	
Cocktails	£6.99		Potatoes	£6.99	
Cookies & Biscuits	£6.99		Rice & Risotto	£6.99	
Cupcakes & Fairycakes	£6.99		Salads: Simple, Fast & Fresh	£6.99	
Detox	£6.99		Sauces Salsas & Dressings	£6.99	
Dinner Lamb	£6.99		Sensational Stir-Fries	£6.99	
Dinner Seafood	£6.99		Simple Healthy Meals	£6.99	
Easy Curry	£6.99		Soup	£6.99	
Easy Midweek Meals	£6.99		Stir-fry	£6.99	
Easy Spanish-Style	£6.99		Superfoods for Exam Success	£6.99	
Essential Soup	£6.99		Sweet Old-Fashioned Favourites	£6.99	
Food for Fit and Healthy Kids	£6.99		Tapas Mezze Antipasto & other bites	£6.99	
Foods of the Mediterranean	£6.99		Thai Cooking Class	£6.99	
Foods That Fight Back	£6.99		Traditional Italian	£6.99	
Fresh Food Fast	£6.99		Vegetarian Meals in Minutes	£6.99	
Fresh Food for Babies & Toddlers	£6.99		Vegie Food	£6.99	
Good Food for Babies & Toddlers	£6.99		Wicked Sweet Indulgences	£6.99	
Greek Cooking Class	£6.99		Wok Meals in Minutes	£6.99	
Grills	£6.99				
Healthy Heart Cookbook	£6.99		TOTAL COST:	£	

Mr/Mrs/Ms _____

Address _____

_____ Postcode _____

Day time phone _____ email* (optional) _____

I enclose my cheque/money order for £ _____

or please charge £ _____

to my: ☐ Access ☐ Mastercard ☐ Visa ☐ Diners Club

Card number

Expiry date _____ 3 digit security code *(found on reverse of card)* _____

Cardholder's name _____ Signature _____

* By including your email address, you consent to receipt of any email regarding this magazine, and other emails which inform you of ACP's other publications, products, services and events, and to promote third party goods and services you may be interested in.

You'll find these books and more available on sale at bookshops, cookshops, selected supermarkets or direct from the publisher (see order form page 119).

TEST KITCHEN

Food director Pamela Clark

Test Kitchen manager Kellie-Marie Thomas

Nutritional information Belinda Farlow

ACP BOOKS

Editorial director Susan Tomnay

Creative director Hieu Chi Nguyen

Designer Caryl Wiggins

Director of sales Brian Cearnes

Marketing manager Bridget Cody

Business analyst Ashley Davies

Chief executive officer Ian Law

Group publisher Pat Ingram

General manager Christine Whiston

Editorial director (WW) Deborah Thomas

RIGHTS ENQUIRIES

Laura Bamford, Director ACP Books

lbamford@acpuk.com

Produced by ACP Books, Sydney.

Printed by Dai Nippon, c/o Samhwa Printing Co., Ltd, 237-10 Kuro-Dong, Kuro-Ku, Seoul, Korea.

Published by ACP Books, a division of ACP Magazines Ltd, 54 Park St, Sydney; GPO Box 4088, Sydney, NSW 2001.

Ph: (02) 9282 8618 Fax: (02) 9267 9438.

acpbooks@acpmagazines.com.au

www.acpbooks.com.au

To order books, phone 136 116 (within Australia).

Send recipe enquiries to:

recipeenquiries@acpmagazines.com.au

Australia Distributed by Network Services, phone +61 2 9282 8777 fax +61 2 9264 3278 networkweb@networkservicescompany.com.au

United Kingdom Distributed by Australian Consolidated Press (UK), phone (01604) 642 200 fax (01604) 642 300 books@acpuk.com

New Zealand Distributed by Netlink Distribution Company, phone (9) 366 9966 ask@ndc.co.nz

South Africa Distributed by PSD Promotions, phone (27 11) 392 6065/7 fax (27 11) 392 6079/80 orders@psdprom.co.za

Breads and muffins:

The Australian women's weekly

Includes index.

ISBN 978 1 86396 719 8 (pbk)

1. Cookery (Bread). 2. Muffins.

I Clark, Pamela. II Title: Australian women's weekly

641.815

© ACP Magazines Ltd 2007

ABN 18 053 273 546

KE   1/08